EVANGELISM
FROM THE
BOTTOM UP

EVANGELISM
FROM THE
BOTTOM UP

WILLIAM PANNELL

ZondervanPublishingHouse
Academic and Professional Books
Grand Rapids, Michigan

A Division of HarperCollinsPublishers

269.2
P194e

Evangelism From the Bottom Up
Copyright © 1992 by William E. Pannell

Requests for information should be addressed to:
Zondervan Publishing House
Academic and Professional Books
Grand Rapids, Michigan 49530

Library of Congress Cataloging-in-Publication Data

Pannell, William E.
 Evangelism from the bottom up / William E. Pannell.
  p. cm.
 Includes bibliographical references.
 ISBN 0-310-52221-8
 1. City churches. 2. City churches–United States.
 3. Evangelistic work. 4. Evangelistic work–United States.
 I. Title.
 BV637.P36 1991
 269'.2'091732–dc20   91-35949
                      CIP

All Scripture quotations, unless otherwise noted, are taken from the HOLY BIBLE: NEW INTERNATIONAL VERSION (North American Edition). Copyright © 1973, 1978, 1984, by the International Bible Society. Used by permission of Zondervan Bible Publishers. Some quotations are the author's translations.

Edited by Michael G. Smith and Robert D. Wood
Cover designed by Lecy Design
Cover photo by Eric Lecy

Printed in the United States of America

92 93 94 95 96 / AK / 10 9 8 7 6 5 4 3 2 1

Contents

Introduction

Urban evangelism has a history that covers more than one and a quarter centuries in North America. By 1860 the major urban centers that anchored the industrial heart of America were well in place—Boston, New York, Philadelphia, Pittsburgh, and Chicago. Right behind them, and rivaling them in strategic location, were the mid-South centers of St. Louis, Cincinnati, Memphis; and in the deep South, New Orleans and Atlanta.

The great revival and evangelistic meetings of Finney and Moody were, for the most part, held in urban settings. Finney's career, stretching from the 1820s to his death in 1895, was more revivalist in nature and reformist in influence and embraced rural and small-town America. But he did not ignore the cities and left his mark on New York, Rochester, and Cincinnati, to name only a few.

The career of Dwight Lyman Moody, the former shoe cobbler from Chicago, was linked with America's urban centers almost exclusively, marking him as this nation's first urban evangelist. At least, the first of the ever-popular and often effective "one-to-the-many" method of proclamation. Moody's crusades at home and abroad were unleashed at the heart of the burgeoning urban centers with their growing industrial clout and pervasive human squalor.

With the Civil War behind it, the nation settled into the tough years of rebuilding. The industrial revolution, propelled by Whitney's gin, had exploded in the North. Energy for manufacturing and other economic enterprise, long stifled by the civil conflict, was released and channeled by American entrepreneurs. Factories were built; others greatly expanded. By the early 1880s the country felt the first waves of migration that were to change the entire ethos of the cities of the East Coast. Europe gave up its tired, its weary, and its poor, and they began streaming into this country so that by 1910 millions had shuffled their weary feet through Ellis Island and Boston. Many of them pushed into the American Midwest. But most of them stayed in the urban centers, supplying cheap labor for the sweat shops and steel mills of the East.

The "Great Barbeque" had begun. There was money to be made. An orgy of industrial expansion carried with it a declension of moral values and human respect. Watered-down stock on Wall Street and dirty politics in Washington set the tone for an America on the make. Millions were made. Other millions were had.

This was the America into which these giants of evangelism and revival came preaching—an America of incredible expansion and energy, of great conflict and optimism, of sprawling frontiers to the west and ever-crowding urban centers throughout the East and the Midwest. These early preachers were followed by numerous others, from Sam Jones to Billy Sunday to Billy Graham. They all majored in preaching to America's urban centers.

Many other Christians did more than preach. As early as 1845 William A. Muhlenberg founded the Church of the Holy Communion in New York City and set up a ministry to the urban poor. He was Episcopalian. Russell Conwell, famous for his lecture, "Acres of Diamonds," pioneered in community-oriented services including gymnasiums, day-care nurseries, and manual arts classes in Philadelphia. Baptists and Methodists developed strong urban programs that sought not only to feed the hungry, but also to offer skills-education for the poor. To be sure, much of this was too middle class in its orientation to allow for a deeper critique of the causes of poverty, but it served notice to fellow Christians that the church had a responsibility to human beings beyond getting their souls saved.

A key debate among urban Christians was over the extent to which Christians and their institutions should involve themselves in social ills. The debate gained momentum after the Civil War, reached its zenith just prior to World War I, then smoldered and died among evangelicals around the early 1930s, and has only recently been resurrected by some of the younger evangelical leaders in North America and their counterparts in the two-thirds world.

In arguments that sound terribly current, some leaders of the late 1800s argued against any ministry that produced or perpetuated what they considered a welfare condition among the poor. Even Washington Gladden, by no means a fundamentalist in theology, while critical of capitalism and corporate oppression of workers, expressed disdain for both the evangelism of Billy Sunday and the "socialists" of the welfare movement.

Another voice in that debate was that of the Salvation Army protesting the inhuman treatment meted out to the poor by charitable agencies. The Army was frequently criticized for its openhandedness with the poor, yet remained committed to a practice of openness toward the most wayward, whether prisoner, vagrant, unwed mother, or prostitute. Furthermore, one of its leaders, Ballington Booth, Commander of the American Salvation Army, claimed in a *New York Tribune* interview that what poor people needed was justice. "We must have justice," he pleaded. "more justice."[1] His remark expressed a developing attitude among some believers to call for a change in the social order itself.

Others, and their names are household words among some evangelicals—A. B. Simpson of the Christian and Missionary Alliance, Florence and Charles Crittendon, J. A. McAuley, Kate Waller Barrett. While not always in harmony with their more radical brothers and sisters, they were nonetheless aware that urban evangelism and social responsibility could not be separated. Many of these workers shared a common theology derived from John Wesley and a common experience warmed by the fires of revivalism. They had also been converted by the city itself, by the squalor and misery of its poor. They knew that holiness of life could not allow suffering and injustice to prevail when it was within the power of God's people to do something about it.

Urban evangelism today, especially in North America and in its more popular forms and public styles, is still based on the Moody model. It is the one-to-the-many approach conducted by the gifted, charismatic preacher with an open, worn, leather-bound Bible in hand. Of course, there are fewer evangelists of this sort about, and only a handful who can marshal the forces necessary to stage major evangelistic events in any city. And those events are rarely held in the central cities. The tactic today is to stage a major crusade near a major central city, say in Pontiac (but they will call it a Detroit Crusade), and televise it to the rest of the country. But old-fashioned religion southern-style, even when aired on television, is merely a camp meeting with air conditioning. Its style and ethos are calculated to reach people who have already been reached and are in harmony with the style and message of the preacher.

More encouraging is the movement on the part of some churches, a few seminaries, and various lay people to take American cities seriously. Curriculum offerings, field assignments, urban training institutes, and church growth strategies for all kinds of people have sprouted in the past several years. These phenomena suggest a new day for evangelism in the urban centers. Most of this new energy comes from Anglos, who, like sleeping giants, are stirring to respond to a new urban reality.

The reality to which they are responding is that (according to 1980 census figures) seventy-five percent of all Americans now live in cities. (The figures are based on a United States Bureau of Census definition that includes all persons living in an urbanized area and all persons outside of urbanized areas living in places of 2500 or more.) Nearly eighteen million Americans live in that corridor of cities stretching from Boston to Washington. From there one can move around the country from city to city and witness similar urban trends and configurations, though on smaller scales in most regions. These growing urban clusters signal the direction and movement of America's future. It is toward the cities. The census figures reflect a global urban reality. The world has gone urban. The number of people living in cities today outnumber the entire global population 150 years ago. Mexico City, on the brink of becoming the world's largest city, now encompasses 890 square miles and has swelled to 18 million people. *Time*, in a lead article, cites this urban phenomenon as a worldwide movement of millions of people: Tokyo-Yokohama 17.1 million; São Paulo 15.9 million; Cairo 12 million, Calcutta 10.2 million; Shanghai 11.9 million.[2] It is this global phenomenon that prompted one Roman Catholic missiologist to argue that the city has become a sign of the times. "A process [urbanization] that involves so many members of humankind cannot but constitute a sign of our times and cannot but suggest many indications of God's plans and hence of the specific missionary mandate for our generation."[3]

The city is the proper locus of evangelism today. How, then, can one explain the reluctance of churches and their supporting institutions, especially seminaries, to engage this reality? For one thing, there persists in America a strong anticity bias. Most Americans, given a choice, opt for making a life in the suburbs where they can eke out a compromise of sorts between town and country. Ogden Nash summed up this attitude of many ex-urban Americans to their cities in his terse comment: "The Bronx? No Thonx."

Churches have, both consciously and unconsciously, acted on this bias no less than the unchurched. So it is not surprising that we see large crusades and seminars of various kinds being held, not *in* the major cities, but on their fringes. An event advertised for Washington, D. C., is as likely to be held in Arlington, Virginia, or Columbia, Maryland, as in Washington itself. A seminar planned for Los Angeles may well be staged in Anaheim. And Detroit often means Pontiac or Troy!

The attitude of Americans toward their cities is certainly mixed at best. Philip Slater observed some years ago that "'civilized' means, literally, 'citified.' The attitudes of a culture toward its cities is an accurate index of the culture as a whole.

We Americans behave toward our cities like an irascible farmer who never feeds his cow and then kicks her when she fails to give milk."[4] I recall hearing a leading evangelist argue that it was never God's intention that people live in cities. And I recall the late Hubert Humphrey express the hope that as a result of a national growth policy that he supported "a migration back to the countryside could be triggered" so that people could live "where God intended them to live." The biblical image of humankind living in a garden dies hard in America.

But the Bible does not simply convey the story of a rural and pastoral life for God's people. Human being may have begun in a garden, but human history began in a city.[5] And between the beginnings in Cain's city and the conclusion of human history in the New Jerusalem are all sorts of villages, towns, and cities in the biblical account. The culmination of history is the descent of the city of God from heaven. The strategy of the Spirit has always been to penetrate these towns and cities. A prophet may be recruited while plowing, but he most certainly will deliver his message in the capital city. That's where the politicians and princes are. That's where the buttons, the levers, and the strings are that control the destinies of people in rural parts.

Another reason behind the tendency of some Christians to ignore the city is theological in nature and grows out of the church's captivity to a rural ethos. Much of the church has no theological self-consciousness that would tie it to an urban world. It has no urban theology. This is especially true of the evangelical wing of the church, which struggles to get beyond its captivity to a frontier-rural orientation. This struggle is evident as far back as the early days of the crusade ministry of Mr. Moody. To be sure, the evangelist knew the strategic importance of the city: win the cities and reach the world. But his appeal was primarily to an urban population with rural memories. Historian Martin Marty observes that

> Dwight L. Moody perfected the urban style of evangelism. In many respects his was a re-enactment of rural rites in urban settings. Large elements of his audiences and respondents were middle class Protestants of rural background and not

11

the hardened secularists he implied they were as he issued his calls for conversion.[6]

Marty highlights a significant point. Not only were those audiences rural in ethos, but many were also middle class. Both of those factors inclined evangelism toward a social and cultural conservatism. And cultural conservatism married to a traditional Protestantism does not usually address all the questions posed in an urban setting.

Walter Rauschenbusch discovered this to be true. A pastor in a section of New York City called Hell's Kitchen, the Baptist preacher came to see that nothing he had learned in seminary had equipped him for the struggle for humanness going on in his new "parish." His theological education was in the best tradition of Euro-American scholarship. It was also bourgeois, as captive to middle-class cultural values as were most of the churches of the day. Rauschenbusch's struggle to find a viable theological frame of reference for his work among the dispossessed in urban America led him to find other tools with which to deal with this new frontier. He found them in the emerging social sciences, especially in sociology, and the new disciplines affecting biblical studies.

It was out of one pastor's pain in urban ministry that the church received its first gift of a truly urban theology. It was called the theology of the social gospel.[7] It was as controversial in 1917 as liberation theology is in the 1990s. Both theologies attempt the same thing, to assist the church in dealing with a new context for mission; the city in the first instance, and oppression and deprivation in the second. Rauschenbusch would have understood Gutiérrez.

It has been common for evangelicals promoting evangelism to react negatively to the social gospel mystique. I say mystique because few evangelists and even fewer lay persons have actually read Rauschenbusch and others of the social-gospel movement. But their typical gut reaction to the very term is what prevails. The "social gospel" is what many Christians fear will emerge and overwhelm us if we take the city seriously. A bastardization of the true gospel will result, and, *voila*, we'll all become liberals!

To be sure there were serious flaws in the theology of the social gospel. But the questions raised by Rauschenbusch still persist. How do you think theologically in an urban world? How do you act on your theology in an urban world? How do you shepherd sheep on mean asphalt streets?

A third reason much of the church has not taken kindly to urban ministry is that over the past thirty years most of America's major cities have changed color. And language. And culture. I watched this happen, indeed was part of this happening, for two decades from 1953 to 1973 in Detroit. Long before the riots of the late 1960s occurred, I had successfully integrated two or three neighborhoods, an evangelical ministerial association, and assorted Christian institutions. But "integration" came to mean the time between our first entry into a neighborhood and the final departure of any remaining white person or institution. By 1970 most of what had called itself the evangelical movement in the Motor City was safely relocated in surrounding suburbs. Their former church buildings were occupied by black Christians and a new Protestant presence emerged as the core religious faith in the city.

But that is ancient history. Today the scene is far more complicated. Detroit, for all its symbolic significance as the auto industry's attempt to recover from its colossal mismanagement of product and personnel, is not where history is. History is more symbolically centered in Miami, Houston, and Los Angeles. Los Angeles, as one writer has put it, is the western capital of a region called Mex-America. It is anchored on the other end by Houston. Los Angeles is a different kind of city from Detroit. It is located in a county that splays across 4,083 squares miles. In Los Angeles County there are, besides Los Angeles, eleven cities with populations exceeding 80,000. Including Los Angeles, these dozen cities express themselves in 104 languages. TV station KSCI Channel 18, broadcasts in "14 languages including Farsi, Tagolog, Samoan, and Rung Hee Rung Jaidi, an Indian dialect."[8] It is estimated that there are 130,000 Arab Americans, 200,000 Iranians, 150,000 Armenians

13

and 90,000 Israelis, who now call the southern California area home.

The county's Anglos and its one million blacks now share their territory with some two million-plus Mexicans, 200,000-plus Salvadorans, 50,000 Guatamalans, 44,000 Cubans, 36,000 Puerto Ricans, and perhaps another 50,000 people dispersed from war-torn Central American countries.

The fastest growing population segment, contrary to public opinion and the rantings of many politicians, comes from Asia. Now referred to officially as "Asian-Pacific peoples," they come from twenty Pacific-rim countries. They represent such exotic and disparate countries as Sri Lanka, Burma, Pakistan, Korea, Taiwan, Afghanistan, Vietnam, Samoa, Guam, and the Philippines, to name a major sampling.

Over sixty-seven languages are spoken in Los Angeles public schools, and more are being added. Popular myth aside, Beverly Hills is not all Rodeo Drive. Nearly 40 percent of that city's kindergarten population is enrolled in an English-as-a-second-language program. The city has become a colored city. Since the last census in 1980, Los Angeles County has seen its private school enrollment increase to 200,050. They are mostly white. Public school figures reflect this shift: "26.6 percent white, 20.7 percent black, 50.7 percent Hispanic, 7.7 percent Asian and 0.3 percent American Indian."[9]

Similar trends can be discerned in varying degrees in every major city in America, including Detroit. Clearly these have become different cities from what they were at the outset of white flight in the mid-fifties. It is this drastic change in the complexion and culture of the city that constitutes the new challenge for mission in the city. Many, if not most, of the newer people have little or no contact with the institutions that have seen themselves as the keepers of the evangelistic flame. A Vietnamese would have had a greater chance to meet an evangelical had he stayed home than he does by moving to the north side of Chicago.

The city has become "colored." This is significant because those who have assumed responsibility for evangelism in North America—indeed the world—are predominantly white. Many of them still function under the seductive control of America's reigning ideology of white supremacy. Of course evangelicalism is not exclusively white in its cultural orientation any more than America is. But it is still true that while evangelicalism does not like to consider itself white in its orientation, it, like the society as a whole, is careful to keep it that way. Black Americans have referred to this as the "rightness of whiteness" doctrine, or ideology, and its most recent expression is the best-selling volume saluting Western culture, *The Closing of the American Mind*. The book is widely quoted among evangelical leaders to defend, however unwittingly, an ideology of white cultural supremacy. This sets up a fascinating set of questions for evangelism in the years ahead.

For instance, will the evangelical church get beyond its current enslavement to the ideologies of white supremacy and engage nonwhites in a ministry of reconcilation? Can the churches in the city and in the suburban rings around the city find ways to cooperate in mission beyond the token salute often associated with the annual pastors' swap during Brotherhood Week? Will the seminaries take the urban world seriously and begin to prepare men and women for ministry in this context at home and abroad? In a typical city of more than 100,000, where many cultures are not only present but compete for power, how does the church live out its profession to be a "reconciling" church?

If the first assumption of this book is that the world has gone urban, the second assumption at work is that evangelism cannot be separated from ethics.

All human activity is subject to ethical judgments. Ethics is intertwined with religion. And religion is at the core of all culture, shaping and directing the shared meanings of a people. As people interact and give expression to their values and concerns, their religion and their ethics become profoundly social. This has always been true even though anthropologists have only recently begun to make any headway in convincing a secular society to take note of it. The Scriptures know of no culture that is not religious at its core and no religious experience that is not social in its meaning and expression.

In the Judeo-Christian faith, God reveals himself to be a holy God, and his intentions for his covenant people are that they too be holy. From this source in the nature of God proceeds the scriptural emphasis upon justice. It is God's clear intention that his covenant people be like him in holiness and justice. These are marks of his people's faithfulness to him and their identity with him.

Not only is holiness a divine expectation for believers of all ages, but it is also the basis of a radical social ethic. As Jesus put it, all the commandments can be summed up in one's love of God, oneself, and one's neighbor. And the most scathing denunciation from the prophets, from Jesus, and from the apostles fell on those who trivialized this ethic by making it a private affair between themselves and God or spiritualized it so as to avoid its social implications.

Christians are usually aware of the biblical teaching on love of neighbor and obligations of justice and mercy. But in recent history, at least for the past century, the emphasis in conservative, evangelistic circles has been upon those ethical problems that are usually understood to be personal ethics. It is increasingly clear today, however, that individual or personal ethics cannot stand apart from social or corporate ethics.

Around the world little people—people who lack visibility, stature in the world, power—are being oppressed, not only by other little people, but by people in high places. One need only mention South Africa, the Sudan, Romania, Chile, or the Philippines to make the point graphically. Or, if we bring the issue into the national arena we Americans know best, what about the U.S.A. and the U.S.S.R.? To include the Soviet Union and the United States in the same breath seems blasphemous to many. Nonetheless, from the bottom up, they are both guilty of corporate crimes against the powerless.

The globe has become one huge ethical case study. Moral myopia and justification of evil replicate themselves easily in a world that defines justice as self-interest. All the nations, because of their economic, political, and military intentions, are part and parcel of this ethical morass. And here's the kicker: not one of the nations is devoid of strong religious sanctions for its actions. Even the Soviet Union, with its previous official denial of religion, had elevated its ideology to the place of religion in its national life. It remains to be seen what a return to traditional religious expression will bring to the masses in Eastern Europe and the Soviet republics.

The task of evangelism is to proclaim the gospel in the face of this global human ethical malaise. Despite the trendiness in our culture of new forms of superficial "humane" behavior, the old sins have not vanished. Racism, militarism, nationalism, sexism, and religious triumphalism have simply donned new attire and acquired a new vocabulary. None of them, however, has given up its desire for power and dominance over the peoples of the earth.

Even deeper than my concern about the relationship between evangelism and social ethics is my concern about the relationship between evangelism and theology. For the church must proclaim its message today in a society largely devoid of norms on which to base its ethics. Life in North America is often propelled and redirected by therapy, most of it "pop." In such a culture what matters is self-fulfillment at one end of the spectrum and feeling good at the other.

While society as a whole might be expected to live by therapeutic rather than theological values, it is more troubling that the church is not much different. Especially if one listens to religion programs on television, it is clear that evangelists are not much bothered about theology. While they may preach some theological doctrines, they do not subject their enterprise to theological analysis.

Just as evangelists are often indifferent toward theology, it is clear that theologians are often indifferent toward evangelism. At a few theological seminaries are faculty who have spent nearly a lifetime in evangelistic practice. But they usually do not enjoy the respect of their "more academic" colleagues. Some of the criticism that each has for the other may be justified, or at least sensible. But when things are weighed in the balance, evangelists have always expressed more theology than the academicians would admit. The problem is that much of the theological thinking has not been well conceived; it has not

17

been thought through and is not systematic, that is, it is not academic enough. But, then, if it had been, who would have listened? Thus, the debate has raged. It is a debate we can no longer tolerate. Theology must inform evangelism and must be the bedrock of its entire enterprise. And evangelism must be a serious exercise in theological ethics.

Perhaps an illustration will help clarify my concerns. In 1968, after several years as a minor executive with Youth For Christ, I joined a young black evangelist from Harlem. Following his leadership and alongside other believers, I helped shape what came to be known as Tom Skinner Associates. My first engagement with Associates was an evangelisitic crusade in the city of Newark, New Jersey.

We had been invited by a duly organized group of that city's evangelical fellowship—at least, the part of it that had not left the city for the relative safety of nearby suburbs. It was also a group that defined itself and its task in narrow terms. These people were evangelical because they were evangelistic and theologically conservative. The keystone of their theology was that humankind was sinful and that all the ills of society were the direct result of human sinfulness. Jesus had died to provide the antidote to that sinfulness. If men and women, individually, would receive the proffered gift of the gospel, those social ills would be cured. The problem was individual sinfulness. The cure was individual conversion.

Well, we believed in some of that, too. Except that we had begun to realize that this analysis of society's maladies was seriously flawed. It was sociologically, politically, and, most especially, theologically naïve. But the meetings served then, and sadly, would serve today, as a parable of evangelism in the city.

On the one hand, there was the remnant of a once strong, triumphant evangelical presence, hoping, almost desperately, that an evangelistic campaign for Greater Newark would restore order and sanity to that war-ravaged community. On the other hand, there was that other, invisible Christian presence. These people, because of their traditional noncompliance with the agenda of the sponsoring evangelicals, were excluded from the planning of the series. They included some outstanding evangelicals, and they saw the complexity of the community and its needs. They were often more realistic about the city and its politics, ethnicities, injustices, etc., than the sponsoring group. But they did not always articulate the gospel in the acceptable evangelical manner.

Then there was the organization we represented, a black evangelistic association, caught in the middle. We were naïve, too. In the first place, we did not realize the degree to which, by virtue of our blackness, we represented the ethical issue in that city. Blackness was precisely the reason that city and other American cities burned in the mid-1960s. America was becoming, in the words of the Kerner Report, a country of haves and have-nots, separate and unequal. Secondly, we were naïve about the gospel. We knew, but didn't know we knew, that the gospel was God's final, ultimate antidote to the races' moral dilemma. We knew, but did not see clearly the ramifications of that fact. That is, we did not see the social dimension of that gospel, a dimension not to be confused with the so-called social gospel. Furthermore, we had not seen then that the city itself was the context of humankind's ethical dilemma.

In this regard, the Black Power Conference, convened the year before, was far more knowledgeable. Anyone who examines that report and weighs its recommendations realizes that the black power advocates saw the city to be the focus of a major ethical issue: power and its use. Had we been able to assess this important convocation with the seriousness it deserved, we would have been better equipped to address the most important theological/ethical question of the 1960s: "How does the church preach the gospel, which is the power of God, to the cities, which are the staging grounds for a clash between people with 'conscienceless power' and the majority people with 'powerless conscience?' "

It is doubtful that such a crusade would be held today. If it were, the same issues would still be there. Indeed, since the '60s, politicians have decided to wage war on those very cities, those very people. And there are fewer evangelical churches in those cities now than a quarter of a century earlier. (Of course, I am defining "evangelical churches" in purely WASP [white Anglo-Saxon Protestant] terms. As the reader well knows, such a definition is not adequate nor accurate, but it helps, for the moment, to make my point.)

You can see from this brief sketch that evangelism, in my experience, has become welded inextricably to ethics. But I would argue not only from experience, but also, and more importantly, from Scripture. If evangelism is the means by which a holy God offers forgiveness to a fallen race, then the good news is intended to address the bad news of a profound sinfulness. The sin of Adam and Eve was no mere lapse of memory, no simple maladjustment of their glandular structure. A sinner is a rebel, an unbeliever, an anarchist. We are alienated in mind, enemies of God, full of wicked works. This is old Adam—still alive and dragging us toward death even at the end of the second millennium after Christ. It is no small wonder then that culture in general, social and political systems, and interpersonal relationships share the same diseases and manifest the same symptoms. It should be no surprise to us what evil we witness in our cities. The human race needs to be converted. Of this there is no doubt. But are we not to assert the same thing for the institutions through which injustice is meted out to the powerless?

The way home begins at the point where the good news is heard and repentance takes place. Here begins the ethical encounter (Luke 3:1–14).[10]

Now, you have some idea of the direction in which this volume is headed. Admittedly, this is not a how-to book. But I think "practical" material is here. It is my firm conviction that the best theory is the best practice. Evangelism in North America does not suffer from too much theory. It suffers from too little theory, and this accounts for the statement expressed years ago by the wily old Baptist evangelist, Vance Havner. Observing the church in America he remarked, "We may be many, but we ain't much." As long as technique prevails over theory and growth over ethics, there will be no significant change in that assessment.

My hope in this writing is to make some contribution to the

ongoing debate about the glorious enterprise called evangelism. This is not exhaustive. It may be deemed too sketchy. But it is offered in the hope that it will enhance our understanding of the opportunities that are at our doorstep and point the direction our thought must take if we are to maximize the opportunities given to us.

NOTES

[1]Norres Magnuson, *Salvation in the Slums: Evangelical Social Work, 1865–1920*, ATLA Monography Series no. 10 (Metuchen, N. J.: Scarecrow Press, 1977), 165.

[2]*Time*, August 1984.

[3]Benjamin Tonna, *The Gospel for the City*, trans. William E. Jerman (Maryknoll, N. Y.: Orbis, 1982), xv.

[4]Philip Slater, *The Pursuit of Loneliness: American Culture at the Breaking Point* (Boston: Beacon, 1970), 9.

[5]See Jacques Ellul's explanation in his *The Meaning of the City*, trans. Dennis Pardee (Grand Rapids: Eerdmans, 1970), 6.

[6]Martin Marty, *Righteous Empire* (New York: Dial, 1970), 162.

[7]Walter Rauschenbusch, *A Theology of the Social Gospel* (New York: Abingdon, 1945).

[8]Laura Meyers, "The L. A. Files," *Los Angeles Times Magazine*, April 1984.

[9]Ibid.

[10]Luke 3:1–14.

1

The Meaning of Salvation Today

In his fine book calling for a "new concept in the theory of development," Dennis Goulet states his conviction that

> for developed and undeveloped societies alike basic questions are neither economic, political, nor technological, but moral. What is the good life and what is the good society in a world of mass technology and global interdependence? Is fullness of good compatible with abundance of goods? Is human development something more than a systematic combination of modern bureaucracy, efficient technology, and productive economy?[1]

The question is from the twentieth century and there are obvious differences between our society and the one in which Jesus lived. In his time, there was no mass technology, no bureaucracy, no sense of "global interdependence." Yet then, as now, it was clear that whatever the good life was it was crucially related to morality. This was true in Rome and even more so in Palestine. The Jews were already rooted in a tradition characterized by strong moral and ethical norms.

Then Jesus came to shed new light on the way people ought to behave toward one another. The new order he came to inaugurate was to be characterized by righteousness and equity (Matt. 5:20; Rom. 14:17). His was a spiritual movement based on the principles of Moses and the prophets, but pushing beyond the older law. Its fundamental social ethic was grounded in love, which, the Teacher said, would distinguish his followers from those who followed other gurus (John 13:35).

His was also a movement of the Spirit. God would put a new spirit in his followers and forgive their sins. There would be born a new humanity and a new community where love and mercy would prevail. Those who followed the Way would become like the God whom they followed (Luke 6:27–36). These were the elements of God's development program. Christ clearly intended his disciples to become transformed people and to form transformed and transforming societies. He intended that they *be* moral and not simply deal out futile moralisms. The word for this transformational work of the Holy Spirit is *salvation*.

The term salvation is problematic for many people in the church. For most evangelical Christians the word usually suggests a personal relationship between the believer and God. It is synonymous with being "born again." Thus, in a good testimony meeting, we hear praise to God for "my salvation." Such an experience is valid and testifies to an important truth. Salvation is intensely personal. The Scriptures are full of the stories of men and women who were personally singled out by the Spirit of God and wonderfully saved.

This personal aspect of salvation is seen as a response to the grace of God. It is a matter of "choosing Christ" in contrast with the notion that one could somehow be a passive or accidental Christian, someone merely religious—belonging to a religious system—but not yet a believer in Jesus Christ as Lord. There is confrontation in this personal-relationship dimension of salvation: one is personally wooed by a loving Savior and persuaded by the Spirit of God to renounce a former loyalty and capitulate to the claims of a new and benevolent Lord. To be sure, the ways in which this occurs are many, and the initial effect varies. But there is usually some aspect of this personal experience of God that is included in the term salvation.

It is this very quality of the personal encounter with God that shapes the traditional conservative missiological and evangelistic methodology. By whatever name it is called, this methodology is some form of *personal* evangelism. In an old gospel song I used to sing we heard this refrain, "So you win the one next to you, and I'll win the one next to me." We heard it sung with the conviction that by such means the world would eventually be won. The sentiment was laudable, the logistics mind-boggling, and the enterprise, at times, naïve.

This naïveté has been superseded by more sophisticated methodologies informed by the social sciences. As a colleague assured me recently, the state-of-the-art missiology of our times makes use of "people-groups" strategy and attempts conversion of entire tribes from within. This seems to have biblical precedence also. Salvation in Israel was more a family or tribal affair than something merely personal. Salvation history unfolds through the twelve families of Israel, even though not everyone in the family personally knew the Lord.

A change takes place in the New Testament as the door is opened to the Gentiles. The tribal structure of Israel recedes into the darkness surrounding Calvary, and in the light of resurrection day the offer is made to whosoever will (Rom. 10:12–13). Yet the relationship between the tribe and the individual remains intact, a fact not easily grasped in a society such as ours where individualism is the reigning cultural value. It is tough to evangelize a Jew as long as he is an integral part of the cultural organism.

In spite of the reality of family, clan, and tribe, the typical thrust of evangelism is toward the individual and the typical assumption motivating evangelism is that salvation is fundamentally, if not exclusively, a personal matter.

This singular emphasis on the personal aspect of salvation is seen in the language of the Lausanne Covenant. According to Section 9 of the document, which is captioned "The Urgency of the Evangelistic Task," "the goal should be, by all available means and at the earliest possible time, that every person will have the opportunity to hear, understand, and receive the good news" (p. 6). Thus when evangelicals shout, "Let the earth hear his voice," they really mean "every person."

This individual focus of the gospel colors and limits the definition of salvation. Such a focus owes as much to its cultural origins among Western evangelists as it does to careful biblical exegesis. Without denying the legitimate biblical emphasis on personal salvation, it is clear that individual conversion does not exhaust the meaning of the term. After all, sin is more than a personal matter. It has profound social, economic, and political dimensions. Can salvation cover any less territory than the ravages of sin? Evangelicals agree that salvation does, indeed, have a broader meaning than the personal, but when they are pressed to apply this understanding they tend to allow it to disappear into the abstractions of theological discourse or be batted about at another international convocation where the participants manage to talk the issues to death.

The broader dimensions of the term have been captured by the so-called liberal wing of the church, notably the World Council of Churches. In so doing they have tended to redefine salvation in socio-political categories. Consequently, from the WCC assembly in Uppsala in 1968 to Bangkok in 1972 the emphasis was on humanization and liberation from "sin and its consequences." The emphasis was on structures as well as on the sins of individuals. Salvation was defined in terms of "the liberation of individuals from sin and all its consequences," and the Council called upon the church to fulfill its mission to "call men to salvation in Jesus Christ . . . and to be constantly re-created in his image, in an eschatological community which is committed to man's struggle for liberation, unity, justice, peace and fulness of life."[2]

In its more recent statement on the mission of the church, the language is less oriented toward socio-economic and political categories, but it is still expressive of a broader understanding of salvation than one finds in the Lausanne statement or in any post-Lausanne statements coming from evangelical authorities.

Roman Catholic missiologists and theologians encounter tensions and confusion over the definition of salvation as well. In his Apostolic Exhortation called "Evangelization in the Modern World," Pope Paul VI defined salvation as "God's great gift which consists not only in deliverance from all that oppresses men but especially in deliverance from sin and the Evil One, together with the joy of knowing God and being known by Him, of seeing Him and of resting trustfully in Him." The pope identifies salvation with the reign of God or the kingdom, and observes that "the kingdom and its salvation [key words in the preaching of Jesus Christ] are available as a gracious gift of mercy to any and every man."

It is clear that the Exhortation is person-centered. (It is unfortunate that its language is so sexist throughout.) In this regard, it differs little from the Lausanne Covenant, yet is stronger than the WCC mission statement. But in its attempt to define evangelism, the Exhortation reveals a more comprehensive understanding of salvation than does its Lausanne counterpart. In this regard it is more in harmony with the statement from the World Council. For instance, the Exhortation goes on to say,

> If, then, we must attempt to summarize the meaning of evangelization, we will be more truthful and accurate in saying that the church evangelizes when she strives, solely by the divine power of the message she proclaims, to transform the hearts of each and every man, along with their activities, their lives, and their whole environment.

It is this last phrase that expresses the distinctiveness of the definition. Elaborating on this phrase, the pope stresses the importance of the word "transformation" as follows:

> We speak of transforming every sphere of the human. The church is not interested merely in preaching the Gospel in ever wider geographical areas and to ever larger multitudes of man. She wishes to touch and transform, by the Gospel's power, all the standards of judgment, the reigning values, the interests, the patterns of thinking, the motives and ideals of mankind which are in discord with God's word and His plan of salvation.[19]

This is a bold assertion, and the implications are far-reaching. And in order to assure that this understanding of God's plan of salvation does not go too far, the pope offers certain qualifications. These qualifications are aimed specifically at third-world Catholics whose watchword is liberation. The pope acknowledges the contributions of bishops in the third world who passionately argue for the deliverance of their peoples from oppression; he acknowledges that the offer of salvation "cannot be complete . . . unless account is taken of the reciprocal links between the gospel and the concrete personal and social life of man." [29] Thus the gospel must be addressed explicitly and be adapted to every situation affecting people as individuals and in groups. And "finally it must be a message, especially strong and pointed today, of liberation." [29]

However, the pope makes it clear that the true gospel of liberation does not condone violence or revolution. These, he claims, are not "in accord with the Gospel . . . not Christian." [37] Lest his people apply the definition to the overthrow of unjust structures, he argues that "sudden or violent changes of structures would be deceitful, would be ineffective of themselves, and certainly would not be in conformity with the dignity of the people." [37] The document, like most church documents, including the Lausanne Covenant, is partly political in nature. But this one is aimed at putting liberation theologians and lay activists in their place. The pope seems to be saying that no amount of Bible quoting or theologizing in the interest of developing a "theology for our times" will be acceptable if it omits the essentially spiritual character of salvation—"the establishment of justice in charity . . . and the winning of eternal salvation and blessedness in God as a final goal." [35]

It is not always easy to sort out the meaning of all these words. And these are merely excerpts of what some missiologists conclude are some of the most far-reaching theological and missiological changes in the last hundred years of Roman Catholic missions. But if read from a village in El Salvador or the wasted lands of South Africa, how would they read? How would any of this material, from whatever source, read from a woman's point of view? For all practical purposes, does the Apostolic Exhortation speak about salvation in essentially the same way that the Lausanne Covenant does?

The pope makes clear that there are some things about salvation that are "essential" and certain other aspects that are "secondary." That which is essential is not "purely immanent salvation, measured by material or even spiritual needs which relate solely to man's temporal existence," but is rather a "salvation which reaches far beyond these limited concerns and involves a communion with the sole Absolute, that is, with God . . . it is, therefore, transcendent and eschatological; while it begins in this life, it culminates in eternity."

As it stands, this is a statement most Christians could support. But what, then, according to the document, is "secondary" to salvation? A careful reading, especially in light of the internal politics involved, suggests that the church's duty to proclaim "the liberation of millions of human beings . . . helping the process of liberation get underway, of testifying in its behalf and of working for its completion" [30]—this is secondary. It is a task of the church not unrelated to evangelization, but it is not evangelization. It is, apparently, not part of the "specifically religious aim of evangelization." The reason these two related enterprises are separated is that essential aspects of the gospel deal with the more specific religious and theological meanings of the faith, whereas secondary matters deal with matters which are by their very nature, temporal and imminent.[3]

This terrain is slippery. Perceptions of the essences of salvation are clouded by ideologies anywhere along the spectrum from left to right. Thus terms like "revolution" or "liberation" can become trendy; today's radical is tomorrow's Uncle Tom. Terms get co-opted and bastardized, packaged like a Chopin waltz to sell hamburgers. They are used by heads of Christian organizations to huckster their latest book on changing the world, often a rehash of tried-and-true clichés calculated to soothe donors or support recruitment. Yet such terms can be useful. When they describe social reality, or merely a perceived social reality, they are to be taken seriously.

John Howard Yoder, Mennonite scholar, argues that while the biblical concept of salvation is not congruent with the concept of revolution so current in much of the world's rhetoric, nevertheless salvation must respond to the questions for which revolution seems to be the solution. Decrying the tendency among many churches to reduce its mission to individual dimensions, Yoder writes:

> . . . but for Jesus . . . the basic human problem is seen in less individualistic terms. The priority item for Jesus . . . is not mortality or anxiety, but unrighteousness, injustice. The need is not for consolidation or acceptance but for a new order in which men may live together in love.[4]

Yoder is clear in his insistence that revolution, from a human standpoint, is not salvation. But he is especially helpful in contending that insofar as revolution is the judgment of God upon the existing order, then salvation must speak to that movement. "What most men mean by 'revolution,'" Yoder says, "the answer they want, is not the gospel, but the gospel, if it is to be authentic, must so speak as to answer the question of revolution."[5]

From this pregnant insight Yoder goes on to write about God's original revolution, centering his exegesis on the text of the Magnificat. Here the language is less that of a young Jewish teenager telling her personal story at a midweek prayer meeting than the prophetic telling of the forthcoming deliverance of her people. She praises God for a salvation that sounds very much like the creation of a new social order. The proud are scattered, the power brokers are dethroned, the rich are banished. In their place the poor are exalted, and the hungry are filled with good things (Luke 1:46-55).

In the same chapter Luke goes on to report how Zechariah is filled with the Spirit and celebrates a similar vision of a transformed social order: salvation [deliverance] from the rule of oppressors and hatemongers, forgiveness of sins, restoration to a place of service to God and the nations (compare Luke 1:46-55; 67-79). This is clearly a salvation hope broader than one's own personal need for meaning or self-fulfillment.

Commenting on Jesus' announcement of the inbreaking kingdom of God in Mark's gospel, F. F. Bruce asserts that "these words express, among other things, the assurance that an ardently desired new order, long since foretold and awaited, was now on the point of realization," and "the general implication of the announcement was plain: the time had come when the God of heaven was to inaugurate the indestructible kingdom which would supersede all other forms of world dominion."[6]

The activist/scholar Dennis Goulet claims that the matter of human and national development needs to be centered in a normative question around which any human enterprise can be discussed. For Goulet this question is "What are the requirements of the good life and the good society in a modern world?"[7] The disciples of Jesus would no doubt reply that the answer in a modern world is the same as in a pre-modern society. The requirement of the good life is the transformed life and a good society is one where the principles of justice are observed among its people.

This is the critical vision, the vision that can make a difference. It suggests a new order superseding all other orders that seek world dominion. The promise is terribly, almost painfully, appealing. It is the central vision of Jesus' ministry. It is the central meaning of Calvary. It is the focus of all the celebrating in the book of Revelation. It is a captivating vision.

THE CROSS AND SALVATION

This vision of the good society captivated the apostle Paul. It comes through, strangely enough, in his theology of the Cross. I have been fascinated for years with Paul's use of the Cross in his correspondence with the Corinthian believers. In Palestine, where the primary events of salvation took place, in Rome (and all her far-flung empire), where crucifixion was used to execute the worst of criminals, and in Corinth, where the message of salvation was now being preached—this much was certain: the Cross would be an offense.

Things have not changed. It is still an offense. One evening in a major city in America I had finished preaching and was talking with several people on the platform. The remarks they were making about the sermon were uniformly positive although mixed with curiosity about our mission at the local university. I was in that place as part of a team of persons invited by a coalition of campus ministries. We would fan out

31

over the campus in the coming week to carry out an evangelistic mission.

But as the small knot of people dispersed, I became aware that I was being stalked. The stalker exhibited the signs of being an offended saint and had all the charm and warmth of a wounded bear. "Appearances are often deceiving," I reminded myself, and bade good-bye to the last of the original group. The stalker was next in line. We were finally alone and I discovered that my fears were justified. He was angry and offended. He was especially upset by my application of the text of 1 Corinthians 1.

I had taken my text from the verse that, in the King James Version, comes to its conclusion as follows: ". . . to bring to nought things that are" (v. 28). A memorable phrase in the KJV, but apparently nonthreatening. That evening, however, I had read from The New English Bible. The expression there is laser sharp: "to overthrow the existing order." With tongue in cheek, but still taking that text seriously, I had said that this was our mission at the university during the week.

My brother heard me out of his narrow political mind-set and assumed I was a left-leaning evangelical committed to "domino" theology. After all, if we could advocate the overthrow of the intellectual underpinnings of a major university, and all in one week, we would likely advocate something really radical—like putting fluoride in the water. There may well have been others in that large congregation who felt as he did, even though he and they would have no problem with a generic theology of the Cross. Nor would they object to the preaching of the Cross. Indeed, my offended brother did not object to my preaching of the Cross in general, but rather to my suggestion that the Cross was somehow subversive of white middle-class cultural values.

My assumption then—in the late '60s and early '70s—and now, is that the starting place from which to critique the values of any culture or from which to evaluate any proffered panacea, is the Cross. Here, Jesus said, was "the judgment of this world." Here, the apostle Paul would argue later, was the place where the believer was crucified to the world and the world to the believer (Gal. 6:14). It was the cross of Christ that Paul planted in the midst of a decadent city and in the center aisle of a carnal charismatic congregation. The Cross is the starting point around which "gathers all the light of sacred story." Here is the revelation of God's "foolishness" in the face of humanity's "wisdom"; God's "weakness" in face of humanity's "strength" (1 Cor. 1:18–25).

Bishop Lesslie Newbigin puts the matter in expansive dimensions:

> Our faith is that the Word of God is in truth the power of God unto salvation—not just the rescue of each one of us separately, but the healing, the making whole of the whole creation, and the fulfilling of God's whole will. Our faith is that the cross is in truth the only event in human history which can properly be called the crisis of human history and that the issue raised there for the human race is one beside which even the survival of human civilization on earth is secondary.[8]

The issue raised here is salvation, "the healing, the making whole of the whole creation," and that issue is indeed broader than the saving of each person separately. From the vantage point of Calvary, all creation is reconciled to God in Christ (Col. 1:19–20), all sins are forgiven, principalities and powers are exposed as imposters and dethroned, and vain intellectualisms are ridiculed as "high-sounding nonsense," (Col. 2:8, PHILLIPS).

By now it should be clear: *the Cross stands for God's judgment of the world and all its systems, ideologies, stratagems, and processes that exalt themselves over Christ and his kingdom.* It is judgment against human sinfulness—all aspects of sin, individual and corporate. It is the single most effective and conclusive argument for God's insight into the human condition. "All have sinned and fall short of the glory of God" (Rom. 3:23).

The Cross lays bare the heart of the problem, the human heart. Here is verified the scriptural statement that the heart is deceitful above all things and desperately wicked. Indeed, so profound is the reality of sin that even the prophet wonders who can know its depths (Jer. 17:9). Jesus was bold and unwavering in his exposé of the heart. Making a distinction

33

between what goes into a person and what comes from within, Jesus claims that it is that which comes from the person that makes him or her unclean: "What comes out of a man is what makes him 'unclean.' For from within, out of men's hearts, come evil thoughts, sexual immorality, theft, murder, adultery, greed, malice, deceit, lewdness, envy, slander, arrogance and folly" (Mark 7:20–22). Notice that Jesus called these behaviors "evils" (v. 23), and claimed that they defile people.

The distinction Jesus makes is important. He lived among a people who, many of them, at least, seemed to ignore personhood in favor of scribal traditions. What was important to them was the correct procedure for washing hands before eating or the precision with which dishes and other utensils were readied for use. Such a preoccupation with tradition effectively shifted the emphasis of religious life from dedication to God from the heart to perfunctory worship based on these scribal regulations (Mark 7:6–8). In the process the Word of God was nullified in favor of the precepts of men.

Jesus distinguishes between the man, that is, the person, and the body. The body has certain normal functions: it ingests food, for instance, and eliminates the food it ingests. That process, Jesus argues, never touches the person. Thus nothing entering into a person's body defiles that person because it enters the stomach and not the heart. What defiles the person, Jesus said, is what comes out of that person, from within, from one's self. Human defilement is an inside job. The human heart is corrupt at its core.

It is also clear from the Scripture that the human heart is rebellious. I have always wished that Adam's sin were smoking a cigar out behind the barn. Or even—ghastly thought—adultery, which, for obvious reasons, would have been difficult. But it was nothing so bad as that. It was only rebellion against the government of heaven. It was only anarchy by Adam against his Creator. True, the Fall was profoundly personal. But it was profoundly political[9] as well. Sin entered the world by one man's disobedience, but that act was also a collective one. Death pervaded that whole human race; all have sinned and come short of God's glory, all have become unprofitable, none is righteous, not one (Rom. 3:10). The condition is alienation, but the core and cause of that alienation is rebellion through unbelief. Adam fundamentally denied God the right to reign over him, a dim echo of a determination hurled into the bloodied face of God's own Son centuries later (Luke 19:14ff.).

But there is another theme running throughout Scripture. It is the leitmotiv of humanity's struggle toward wholeness. The human race is not only alienated from God but from itself as well. The Roman Catholic definition of evangelism refers to this social dimension of the Fall when it asserts that transformation includes "all the standards of judgment, the reigning values, the interests, the patterns of thinking, the motives and ideals of humanity which are in discord with God's Word and his plan of salvation."[10]

This social dimension of salvation is the heart issue in Christ's encounter with the young ruler. After inquiring about eternal life and how it is secured, the man hears Jesus recite key parts of the Ten Commandments. They are those that relate people with people, not those that relate people with God. But it is clear that if one is not in proper relation with people— especially the poor—then one could scarcely be properly related to God.

The reigning values of the young man's life are exposed in the final demand of Jesus that he sell his possessions and give the proceeds to the poor. It is important to see this story and the others in Luke's gospel as relating to the inbreaking of the new order, the kingdom of God announced earlier by John the Baptist and then Jesus. It is a commitment to the King that initiates the reordering of one's life and supplies the power to begin a new life in accordance with the principles of the new regime. This is God's kind of politics, and precisely because it is God's, it is more radical than any other option.

Humanity may have political problems as a consequence of its rebellion against God, but those problems cannot be resolved from a mere political stance. Thus the zealot option was as unsatisfactory for Jesus as is the Marxist or capitalist option for the church today. Transformation is the solitary work

35

of God, and participation with God in this work requires a transformation of the mind in conformity with the values and demands of the new kingdom.

Let me summarize the new perspective that I hope I have been able to convey in the preceeding pages. If we were to consult almost any standard theological dictionary, we would discover the typical biblical and theological terms for salvation. The terms commonly included in an exploration of the topic are rich, indeed, and full of meaning: justification, reconciliation, propitiation, adoption, new birth—and these are only a few. But what is not so easily found in these same sources, and what is so desperately needed, are insights into the meaning of salvation from the vantage point of those who are sinned against. If one begins theological reflection in the barrio and not in the library, other key terms and theological themes suggest themselves. Hugo Assman argues that

> if the state of domination and dependence, in which two thirds of humanity live with an annual toll of thirty million dead from starvation and malnutrition, does not become the starting point for any Christian theology today, even in the powerful and affluent countries, then theology cannot begin to relate meaningfully to the real situation. Its questions will lack reality and not relate to real men and women.[11]

For Assman, the starting point for any understanding of salvation is the condition of oppression under which most of the world exists. This is echoed by the evangelical scholar, Thomas Hanks, who writes:

> Anyone who has read much in the theological classics (Augustine, Calvin, Barth, Berkouwer, et. al.) will recognize that the theme of oppression has received little or no attention there. One might think that the Bible says little about oppression. Furthermore, one searches in vain for the theme in Bible dictionaries, encyclopedias, and the like.
>
> However, when we strike the rock of a complete Bible concordance, to our great surprise we hit a gusher of texts and terms that deal with oppression. In short, we find a basic structural category of biblical theology.[12]

In a world where misery is the prevailing reality—especially among urban populations—our task is clear: to ask the Bible to speak to us from a vantage point below, from the bottom. *We must recover a biblical view of salvation from the bottom up rather than from the top down, as is now the prevailing model.* The task should not be all that difficult. The Bible was written in many situations of misery, deprivation, and need.

The Bible was written, for the most part, out of a people's struggle against oppression. Its story is told from the bottom up. We miss this in our affluent, Western social context because, from our vantage, the Scriptures seem to speak the language of individual salvation, personal comfort, and self-fulfillment. The texts of Scripture seem to offer material for nice devotionals and useful group studies of various kinds. In our typical social settings the Bible is not perceived to be a handbook for a new social order. Yet that is precisely what it is. The reasons for this are several, but chief among them is that the interpreters of most of our biblical texts come from among the privileged elites of the world.

If the church is to teach the nations the "all things" of Jesus, it must begin discipleship training exactly where Jesus did—reflecting on the ways of God as he moves and works among the oppressed.

NOTES

[1]Denis Goulet, *The Cruel Choice: A New Concept in the Theory of Development* (New York: Atheneum, 1971).

[2]Bangkok Assembly, Section III, pp. 102–3.

[3]Numbers in brackets in the several foregoing paragraphs refer to paragraph numbers in Pope Paul VI's Apostolic Exhortation, *Evangelization in the Modern World* (*Evangelii Nuntiandi*).

[4]John Yoder, *The Original Revolution* (Scottsdale, Pa.: Herald Press, 1971), 18.

[5]Ibid.

[6]F. F. Bruce, *The Time Is Fulfilled* (Grand Rapids: Eerdmans, 1978), 16, 20.

[7]Ibid., 111.

[8]Source unknown.

[9]The idea is expressed in a parable of Jesus. Notice that the Lukan account of this spirit of rebellion is in a setting where the kingdom of God, i.e., the reign of God, was expected at any time. See also Luke 19:11, cf. v. 38.

[10]*Apostolic Exhortation,* ¶19.

[11]Hugo Assman, *A Theology for a Nomad Church*, trans. Paul Burns (Maryknoll, N. Y.: Orbis, 1975), 54.

[12]Thomas Hanks, *God So Loved the World* (Maryknoll, N. Y.: Orbis, 1983), 4.

2

Who Changed the Agenda?

The front seat of the Camaro was fittingly comfortable as my host pointed out some of the sights of a Mississippi city. When we drew alongside the imposing structure of one of the city's premier churches, his voice took on a more sombre tone, "We had an interesting meeting in that place a while ago. They had turned some black children away from their school and we went to get an explanation of their position."

"How'd it go?" I asked, confirming that I am a glutton for horror stories.

"Well, the pastor received us into his plush office and, after some initial pleasantries, informed us that it was none of our business; that we had no right coming in there to tell him or the church how to run their affairs. We tried to help him see that the matter was more than a private issue, since we were all Christians."

My host continued, "After some calmer discussion the pastor said, 'Well, we may all be Christians, but the difference between you people and us is that you people emphasize one part of the Gospel and we emphasize another.' So we asked him what that was and he told us, 'Well, you folks emphasize reconciliation and we emphasize evangelism.'"

A story like that needs no comment. The pastor's lack of theological insight explains why his church is still a bastion of white supremacy. But the disjunction between evangelism and reconciliation offered in his attempt to distinguish his church's mission from the mission of other churches is not so strange or isolated as it might appear. Thousands of churches in North America make a distinction between preaching the gospel and reconciliation. What they mean by preaching usually extends to other forms of evangelism such as personal witness and church outreach. By working within such definitions these churches create an adulterated form of evangelism that requires no visible demonstration that reconciliation is at the heart of God's salvific intention.

This estrangement of evangelism from reconciliation reflects a major theological fault. To the apostle Paul, the central focus of the Cross was reconciliation. "God was in Christ, reconciling the world unto himself" (2 Cor. 5:19, KJV). The concern we hear in all of Paul's writings is not that God wants all people merely to hear the gospel, or even that all individuals who hear it come to believe it. Paul's claim is that the open secret of this age (the age in which we are now living) is that, through the gospel, God is calling out from among the nations a people for himself. Furthermore, in Christ (Paul's key phrase) all the barriers to unity among peoples of the earth have been broken down. God has waged a successful war through the Cross so that now Jew and Gentile can celebrate the victory in the fellowship of a new humanity in Christ.

This accomplished fact is the mystery of Christ. The apostle's calling was "to make plain to everyone the administration of this mystery" (Eph. 3:9). God's purpose in Christ was always clear to Paul: ". . . to create in himself one new man out of the two, thus making peace, and in this one body to reconcile both of them to God through the cross, by which he put to death their hostility" (Eph. 2:15–16).[1] Whatever else may be involved in the church's evangelistic task, it was clear that the goal of such evangelism was reconciliation. Any failure to practice reconciliation was viewed as a compromise of the gospel and a sellout of one radical feature of the kingdom to the forces of culture.

But the Mississippi experience is more than a theological matter. It is a worldview problem as well. That can be seen in this dichotomy between evangelism and reconciliation. It reflects a Christian version of a national mood, a mood at once reactionary, isolationist, and antirational.[2] Americans are tired of conflict. They want to get back to the quieter days, days before pluralism and liberalism made shambles of a single, consensual way of life. In this nostalgic dream, black folks are in the cotton fields, women are in bedrooms and kitchens, and homosexuals are in closets.

The public issues dividing the American people are well known and have ranged from concern over abortion to national defense. But at the heart of so much of the debate is a passion for what some scholars call "nativism," a desire to return to simpler days, to a less diverse and less complicated nationhood. The current mood is a reaction against a too-rapid social change. Recently it has become mixed with American racism, a strong antipathy toward the poor, a renewed passion for patriotism, and a strong commitment to the good life defined in economic terms. There is a fear in the air, not only of nuclear war, but also that the nation is losing its identity as a white man's country.

This national mood is a source of great pain for many Christians. Sensitive evangelicals know that the claims of the gospel and the implications of Christ's lordship do not easily translate into sentimental patriotism. After all, if Jesus Christ is Lord, Caesar cannot be. Yet the notions of manifest destiny, of "righteous empire," do not die easily. President Eisenhower, in a fit of campaign nationalism, once exclaimed that "our government makes no sense unless it is founded in a deeply religious faith—and I don't care what it is." Commenting on this later, Will Herberg, a noted scholar in religion and philosophy, said,

> Of course he did care—he would have been much worried if Americans had turned Shintoist or Buddhist. What he didn't care was whether they were Protestants, Catholics, or Jews. Why didn't he care? Because they all say the same thing. What do they say? The American way of life.[3]

In other words, the religion of America is America. It was President Reagan calling the Russians "pagans and barbarians" and theirs "an evil empire." It was the same president giving the fundamentalists the impression that his foreign policy was based on a biblical view of the last days, including references to Armageddon. Many Americans, apparently quite a few, are attracted to these preachments. It reminds them of a time when life was less complicated and when they had a clearer vision of who they are. They are the good guys in white hats. Never mind recent history, never mind the facts of the case. God is clearly for us, for now, and for years to come. He is, as he has always been, our own Uncle Sam.

This mood has been captured in American films during the past several years. The big box-office winners: *Terms of Endearment*, *Tender Mercies*, *Places of the Heart*, *Paris, Texas*, *The River*, and to a lesser degree, *Country*, have celebrated what ostensibly are the key and abiding values in the culture. These values are all associated with rural America and are understood in personal terms. Watching these films, one gets no feel for those larger issues that rack society—the country's unresolved involvement in Central America, catastrophic financial deficits, nor the desperate plight of America's farmers in the broader context of multinational agribusiness and the politicization of food around the world.

But conservative Christians want more than a return to simpler days. They also want a return to a simpler Christian mission. What could be simpler than evangelism, or church growth? Neither of these enterprises is easy; they require skill and much hard work. But they represent a simpler agenda for the church. The grassroots of the church, even in so-called mainline denominations, is fed up with the agendas of its distant and often more liberal hierarchy. The cry is "back to basics." This is not all bad. But at its core is this same sense of frustration with rapid social change and the anxieties that it produces. Actually, not much has changed for the poor, white or black, or for those at the margins of society. Maybe this too is cause for rejection of any notion that evangelism and reconciliation should be united. After all, the liberal crusades led by presidents Kennedy, Johnson, and, to some degree, Nixon, did not produce reconciliation. Those national policies and the attempts to implement them simply did not bring people together.

But of course they were not intended to. The signing of the Civil Rights Act of 1964 and the Voting Rights Act of 1965 had in mind freedom and equality before the law, but neither intended nor required reconciliation. Justice was the point, not reconciliation. Yet the courtroom victories in the late '60s changed more than national policies. The movement that gave birth to those policy shifts, led by the young man from Atlanta, forced reconciliation back on the theological agenda of many denominations. Except it was not heard as reconciliation. It was heard as integration. They are not the same.

Reconciliation is a biblical term, a profound theme deeply resonant in the church's theological tradition. Integration, on the other hand, is an American exercise in myth-making, imbedded deep in the psyche of a nation that has always been embarrassed over the gap between its ideals and its reality. The struggle continues to this day as part of a national exercise in self-definition, and the churches are no clearer on this distinction than is the secular community.

In many ways the tension between integration and reconciliation is still the church's moral dilemma in North America. Integration as a goal for most Americans is dead, having gone the way of court-ordered busing and the last haunting strains of "We Shall Overcome." We didn't and we haven't, but it was time to move on to other things. The issues now are economics and one's place on the rungs of class and social status. As the late Saul Alinsky put it, the trinity most operative in American society is composed of the haves, the have-nots, and the have-a-little-want-mores. The last group is the middle class, and, said the noted gadfly,

> They could be described as social, economic and political schizoids. Generally, they seek the safe way where they can profit by change and yet not risk losing the little they have. Thermopolitically they are tepid and rooted in inertia. Today

in Western society and particularly in the U.S., they comprise the majority of our population.[4]

This view underscores a subtle but significant shift in human relations. The point is that whereas racialism kept people from giving support to the program of integration up through the '70s, today it is more likely to be economic considerations that hold the key. In short, the focus is on class, not race. William Julius Wilson made this very point:

> A new set of obstacles has emerged from basic structural shifts in economy. These obstacles are therefore impersonal, but may prove to be even more formidable for certain segments of the black population. Specifically, whereas the previous barriers were usually designed to control and restrict the entire black population, the new barriers create hardships essentially for the black underclass. . . . In short, whereas the old barriers bore the pervasive features of racial oppression, the new barriers indicate an important and emerging form of class subordination.
> . . . In the economic sphere, class has become more important than race in determining black access to privilege and power.[5]

The shift in emphasis at the national level coincides with the advent of the new conservatism in the 1990s, and is but another step in the evolution of the "Me generation." Commerce and business is a driving motif of American history, so the current passion to make a buck is nothing new. What is new is the intensity and pervasiveness of the cultural revolution at the beginning of the 1990s, which is based on self-interest. The society, as Christopher Lasch argued, is no longer pursuing or driven by a redemptive ethos. The Protestant ethic simply does not influence the culture as it once did—certainly not on weekends. What has taken its place is more akin to psychology than theology, producing a therapeutic society.

> Plagued by anxiety, depression, vague discontents, a sense of inner emptiness, the "psychological man" of the twentieth century seeks neither individual self-aggrandizement nor spiritual transcendence but peace of mind, under conditions that increasingly militate against it. . . . Therapy has estab-

lished itself as the successor both to rugged individualism and to religion.[6]

Fixation on the good life (wealth, career, leisure) is part of this new culture. It is what Elizabeth Drew observed when assessing the political climate in 1984. "In America these days, it appears that helping the poor is out of fashion and an 'I've got mine, Jack' attitude is in fashion."[7] Nothing personal, you understand. No one group is targeted in the old-fashioned manner of the Klan. It's just that God takes care of those who look out for number one—personally or nationally.

Daniel Yankelovitch claims that the revolution is so pervasive as to alter the ethos of America for years to come. Says the noted researcher, "Tomorrow is not going to look like yesterday. In fact tomorrow . . . is being shaped by cultural revolution that is transforming the rules of American life and moving us into wholly unchartered territory."[8]

Both Lasch and Yankelovitch see the same problem in this cultural revolution. They question whether a people can achieve self-fulfillment by placing the self at the center of life. Their critiques are reminiscent of those by Daniel Bell, whose *The Cultural Contradictions in Capitalism* is a classic. Neither economics nor psychology is an adequate center around which a truly valuable life can revolve.

Says Yankelovitch:

> In dwelling on their own needs, they discover that the inner journey brings loneliness and depression. They are caught in a debilitating contradiction: their goal is to expand their lives by reaching beyond the self, but the strategy they employ constricts them, drawing them inward toward an ever narrowing, closed-off "I."[9]

The pursuit of self-fulfillment has had a profound effect on foreign policy. The years from 1968 until now have been tumultuous for the country. Through those years civilization (the USA version, at least) turned another corner. If a single event is needed to identify that pivotal change, it was the storming of the American Embassy in Teheran; the date, November 4, 1979. As the enormity of that drama became clear, this nation, its nerves already frayed, would learn that it was no longer in control of its vital interests in the Middle East.

America was threatened again, not so much in military terms as in psychological terms. Politics became a frantic attempt to restore a rapidly deteriorating self-image. The Ayatollah Rubollah Khomani rubbed Sam's nose in camel dung, and, timing his last indignity to coincide with a national election campaign, helped to topple one president and elect another. By the end of 1980, trees were swathed in yellow ribbon, and Mr. Carter was headed back to Georgia. He took with him an era of liberalism and human rights that was supplanted by a preoccupation with national self-interest. Nationalism is not the most congenial atmosphere in which to promote reconciliation among nations.

But if self-interest would shape American attitudes toward foreign nations, another fact of history would significantly affect the demands for reconciliation at home. An ever-restless and displaced humanity sends streams of refugees from places of conflict and destruction to places of relative peace and stability. Fleeing conditions ranging from war to drought, the human race is increasingly hopeless and rootless, caught up in a desperate flight merely to survive. Many of these people have found their way westward and are now a major cause of alarm in the capitals of Europe and North and South America. It is this new "troublesome presence" that further brings into question this nation's intentions regarding the minorities in her midst. The issue is no longer black and white—it is native Americans in Chicago, Filipinos in San Francisco, Cubans in Miami, Vietnamese in Corpus Christi, and Mexicans everywhere!

The influx is dramatic and, for many Americans, traumatic and threatening. After all, these new faces are different; they are colored. They do not come from stable, predictable, old Europe but from the inscrutable Orient and the emotion-oriented Latin world of Central and South America. They are really not "our kind of people." (One of these days I can imagine one of the East Asian countries, probably influenced by wealthy ex-patriots in southern California, offering to place a statue in the harbor of Los Angeles. But the irony of this gesture of goodwill will be that the statue will depict Americans, not with the recognizable European visage but with distinctive Oriental or Latin features.)

America has been and still is a hyphenated society: Euro-American, Afro-American, Asian-American, Latin-American, to name a few of the common conjunctions. The exceptions to this rule live on reservations and even they are now called native Americans. Furthermore, and I am not sure the scholars will admit this, these hyphenated people, with the significant exception of Afro-Americans, still maintain an intense loyalty to the old country. The new immigrants may be naturalized citizens, but they proudly wave national flags next to Old Glory. The old world prejudices are present in the new setting; ancient rivalries between countries flourish in Pasadena as they did, for instance, in Armenia and Turkey.

Other equally remarkable factors of the past twenty-five years have changed America's views of ethnicity. One was the civil rights movement and the drive toward black solidarity and black power within that movement. Society shook off the black-power movement, preferring to listen to the more moderate preachments of Dr. King and his American dream motif. The more radical elements of the black-power movement self-destructed or were hopelessly splintered by the police tactics of the government. Others were elected to political office.

Dealing with black aspirations in America has become manageable for the social and political leaders who must navigate the swirling waters. The society has over two hundred years of experience in dealing with this troublesome presence. It will not be so easy with the Latino-Asian tide, and that story is only now being written.

Such realities raise questions about the common assumption of America as a melting pot. We see today every ethnic group singing its own praises. "Polish power" bumper stickers appear in Hamtramck, Michigan, and Serbian flags fly proudly in taverns in Cleveland neighborhoods. The Irish in Boston always did fly their banners, much to the discomfort of blacks in Roxbury.

These same historical movements had a salutary effect upon American missiologists, especially those in the forefront of the influential church growth movement. This movement was and is associated with the School of World Mission and the Institute for Evangelism and Church Growth at Fuller Theological Seminary in Pasadena, California. Founded by the late veteran missionary Donald McGavran, the school has made gospel among American churches what McGavran championed in caste-bound India. The influence of this school of thought has been enormous, "far more than any of us laboring at it had dared to ask or think," claimed McGavran. Yet this movement has done more to diminish the biblical mandate for reconciliation and justice among the oppressed than any other Christian endeavor during the last twenty-five years.

Such was not the intention of the church growth movement. At least it was not a stated objective of these leaders to subvert the church's call to set the captives free. Rather, it happened by default. By placing the church's priorities on growth, it played into the waiting hands of American churchmen eager to get themselves and their congregations past the uprisings and disturbances of the Sixties.

The assault upon the broader agenda of the kingdom of God coincided with certain "compulsives" within American culture. A "cultural compulsive," according to one of Fuller's missiologists, is an indication of a culture's temper, and it is the temper of a culture that, often as not, makes an idea catch on. Often the idea is not nearly so important as the general temper of the moment. A cultural compulsive represents the vested interests of the establishment of a given culture.

According to Allan Tippett, compulsives "indicate not the falseness of a theory, but the importance of its social meaning." Quoting V. F. Calverton, an early proponent of the concept of cultural compulsives, Tippett affirms, "The source of power of the cultural compulsive is not the truth or falsehood of the doctrine, but its 'adjustability to other interests.'"[10] Cultural compulsives, while rendering objectivity impossible, are vital to a society. Like tradition, they hold society together, giving it cohesion, meaning, and direction in its social thought. Tippett concludes, "Therefore it is important that we should recognize the cultural compulsives in all social science. Experiments and invention are open for acceptance more when they meet a desperate need. Awareness of the compulsives keeps us discerning, critical and flexible."[11]

Tippett's insight is illuminating. Church growth theory is based upon insights supplied by the social sciences, especially sociology and anthropology. But one suspects that Tippett's recognition that the use of these disciplines be accompanied by discernment of the needs of a given culture has been selectively applied. The Swedish anthropologist Gutorum Gjessing makes a necessary comment upon the responsibility of anthropology to society, "Anthropology, as a social activity, has a responsibility to society; anthropology cannot live in isolation from reality; anthropology must serve humanity ethically."[12]

It would seem fair, in light of these insights, to expect those who take the sciences seriously to be discerning, critical, and sensitive to the ethical implications of their enterprise. They should be held accountable not only for what they say, but also, and sometimes more so, for what they do not say. Social scientists should be judged by their own criteria. Tippett claims as much when admitting that this is in the line with the Great Commission: "Of course, if Christianity does not show a responsibility to society, if she lives in isolation from reality and if she has no world vision, she may be declared irrevelant. That she has fallen under this condemnation cannot be denied, and to this extent we may have ourselves contributed to the build-up of cultural compulsives against us."[12] Indeed, there is ample proof of this in North America.

The reigning compulsives in North America are the passion for self-fulfillment, the search for renewed status as the number-one world power—whether in athletics, military might, or business—and a distinctly American brand of nationalism that seeks validation by religious sanctions. American Christians, often more American than Christian, have been attracted to the church growth movement for a number of good reasons—and a few not so good.

We are a nation of faddists; we do not like to stick with a

problem long. We seek the easy way, accepting what the sociologist Philip Slater calls "the Toilet Assumption—the notion that unwanted matter, unwanted difficulties, unwanted complexities and obstacles will disappear if they are removed from our immediate field of vision."[13]

In the case of the city we move away from the old neighborhood. Out of sight, out of mind. Hence no responsibility for it or for the mess we made of it when we were there. Church growth theory provided yet another way to sanction this American tendency to avoid the unwanted. By arguing that churches grow best within homogeneous groupings, the movement made the more difficult requirement of the gospel, namely reconciliation, unnecessary. At best it is a luxury that can be postponed until there are enough churches to satisfy the Lord of the harvest.

Again this is not the explicit doctrine, the declared ideology of church growth. Nobody connected with this movement, especially McGavran, is against reconciliation or justice for the oppressed. But one looks in vain for these categories in the curriculum.[14] Thus, what is not said constitutes the problem and is the tip-off to the values that are actually held. McGavran argued passionately for justice among the millions of untouchables in India. But when pushed to suggest ways to accomplish this, he argued that only by planting hundreds of churches could this be done. What kind of churches? Reflecting what values? After all, church growth is popular in South Africa also. Would anyone advocate that there should be more of the same kind of churches that are there now?

A further point on American culture: At a deeper level there is a national confusion as to who we are and why we are here. As the late Theodore White saw it, Americans have been searching for America for some years and the search centers on "the nature of the questions Americans ask of themselves, of their purpose in their search to find again an old civility of life and communities in which that civility can reign."[15] The search accelerated in 1980 with the election of a president who seemed to embody all the old virtues long associated with the Puritan ethic—hard work, reverence for the law and authority, apple pie—the fundamentals. But the truth is that there are at least two Americas, the mythical one that many unthinking Americans love to proclaim, and the real one, shot through with denial of the very values it declares.

Philip Slater, while attempting to explain the rift in the culture during the heyday of the counterculture movement, maintains that there are two cultures in America. These are not poorly mixed cultures, that is, not pluralities of different ethnic groups, but two cultures clearly divided along ideological lines. And they are not both playing by the same rules; they are "two growing absolutistic groups with a shrinking liberal one in between, a condition which will obtain until some new cultural structure emerges which is more widely shared." Perhaps no event in recent memory brought this split to the fore more than the reaction within the black community to the nomination of Clarence Thomas to the Supreme Court. The community was split not only between liberals and conservatives, but also, perhaps more importantly, between haves and have nots. Not morality, as in the sixties and seventies, but access to the good life became the major issue. Thus, upwardly mobile blacks joined their white counterparts in saluting Thomas' rise from poverty to the bench. Ideology triumphed over racial and cultural solidarity, and a coalition that had been developing during the Reagan years was further established. What is missing, Slater argues, as these groups attempt mediating strategies, is a moral basis for such mediation.

> So long as our society had a common point of moral reference there was a tendency for conflicts to be resolved by compromise, and this compromise had a moral as well as a practical basis. Today this moral unity is gone, and the only basis for compromise is a practical one.[16]

If this was true in the sixties, it is more true now that the ideological rift has been made the basis of national self-definition. The reigning party in the White House since 1980 has made it clear that to oppose its nostrums is to be un-American. If expedience is the only mediating motivation, then unity is not possible. We remain just what we were during the sixties, a deeply divided society without moral or ethical norms by which to provide a needed unity.

The same divisions exist in the Christian communities in North America. We are divided along ideological lines as firmly as our secular neighbors are. The old guard gravitates toward the old verities, chief among which are evangelism, spirituality (usually defined in individual terms), overseas missions, and currently, a new fascination with signs and wonders in the service of church growth. The new generation, while asserting the values of the older group, asserts the need for a new theological paradigm that will address the core needs of society as a whole. The sad thing about this arrangement is that behind these agendas are ideologies borrowed from a secular orientation.

Evangelism, in this ideological fray, becomes, for the right wing, an exercise in reductionism in order to avoid the larger question of justice. For the left wing, justice becomes the total agenda as it hides the ugly reality of the moral decay in human nature. This is often why groups that major on justice themes are not noted for their evangelistic fervor.

Church growth fits neatly into this scenario. It is an exercise in reductionism. The movers and shakers in the church growth movement are not racists. They are merely reductionists whose preference for church growth expresses a passion to see the nations discipled and to apply their energies to that which works. This has appeal in North America, especially among pragmatic and efficient Yankees in desperate search for something that works and that works effectively. With goals setting, priorities ordering, objectives accomplishing, techniques working, and charts flowing, this has become the American church's number-one growth industry. And now it comes complete with consultants.

By reducing God's agenda to this single priority, church growth leaders are effectively relieved of the necessity to pursue other objectives on the list. Very few of us in the black community doubt for a minute the unwavering evangelical commitment to evangelism. Paragraph four in the Lausanne Covenant will, doubtless, be honored. Since 1974 there have been major conferences and consultations to explore theologies and strategies for evangelization. But will these same people fulfill their commitments to social responsibility? There has been little indication among evangelicals since 1974 that paragraph five would be taken with equal seriousness, as if, in the language of the covenant, they were "both part of our Christian duty."[17] The Lausanne Committee has called no meetings of the scope of Pattaya or Manila to discuss justice and the gospel demand for reconciliation. Instead, they have pursued major conferences proposed and organized by the technocrats of growth.[18] Definitions are important. Whoever controls them sets the priorities. When the term "priority" is included in a definition, its effect is to restrict commitment to the church's total agenda.

By grounding church growth strategy in selective sociological and anthropological categories, the demands of the gospel easily become relativized. After all, this is the same "practical" sociology and anthropology that is used by bankers and realtors to redline whole districts in order to maintain segregated neighborhoods. The villain, they say, has been the appraiser, and he or she operates according to the "neighborhood conformity principles." According to a 1975 training manual of the society of Real Estate Appraisers, this principle recognizes that maximum property values are realized when a reasonable degree of sociological, economic, and psychological homogeneity is present. If an appraiser follows the projections of neighborhood homogeneity and the aging process of a given area, he should be able to manipulate lending institutions to determine who should and should not occupy a given neighborhood. In other words, the single most important concern is growth and stability among homogeneous people. But the system tries to work as if it were amoral, having itself no built-in ethical criteria to apply to the strategy of maintaining inequities and barriers by what appear to be effective principles of growth.

The social sciences can offer much help to the church in clarifying its task and approach to mission in the world. But these sciences are not value-free. At their very core they are not and cannot be in harmony with kingdom values. In a racist society that eagerly pursues the good life at almost any cost, an approach to mission based upon the homogeneous-unit principle is bound to promote some form of redlining. Church growth promotes an ecclesiastical version of this racialist practice precisely because it is predicated upon a so-called value-free social science hermeneutic.

The danger in a hermeneutic grounded in the social sciences is its tendency to absolutize science. The danger is not unlike that great experiment in liberal education at Harvard University. In attempting to move beyond an education that simply served up established dogma, the school sought to establish a new educational framework that would provide a rationale for its continuing commitment to morality and, at the same time, a neutrality or disinterestedness that would permit an authentic encounter with truth. It found it in science. Or so it seemed.

Charles W. Eliot, president of Harvard from 1869 to 1909, had a vision of an emerging America, free from "metaphysical complexities or magical rites," and, according to Silk, he "reinterpreted the '*veritas*' on Harvard's shield, which originally signified Christian truth, to mean the search for scientific truth, which would 'progressively set men free.' "[19] The sort of truth that science is pursuing tends to be an abstraction, one that does not have clear moral and ethical demands. By contrast, Christian truth is ethically colored from the start.

It is this reliance upon a hermeneutic grounded in the so-called "neutral" sciences that threatens to constrict and retard the impact of the gospel in church growth theory and practice.[20] Theology seems to be an unnecessary obstacle to the achievement of the simple objective implicit and explicit in church growth—growth. Consequently, social ethics is largely ignored.

But the hermeneutics of the evangelistic enterprise is critical. I am much impressed by observations made by so-called minorities that one's hermeneutic is usually connected to one's existential circumstance. (Black and brown people, upon hearing that growth has taken priority over ethics and that most of the leaders of the movement are North American Anglos, naturally develop a "hermeneutic of suspicion.") The problem I am getting hold of here can be illustrated by the habit of Lausanne movers and shakers to caption their major events with the "Let . . ." designation ("Let the Earth Hear His Voice," etc.). This pattern only heightens one's suspicion that another form of arrogant cultural imperialism is at work. Who are these people who "let" the earth hear his voice? Viewed from the bottom, evangelism seems to have been captured by an evangelical establishment. It has become institutionalized. It has all the necessary trappings of an establishment: a certified priesthood, accredited schools to ensure continuity among its priests, and an official theology. The maintenance of this establishment guarantees perpetual support from a voluntary constituency. This voluntary support is courted so that, among other reasons, the system can tolerate diversity and encourage the free flow of ideas. It refers to itself as "Christianity today."

The evangelical establishment is global in its outreach. Since the coming of age of the Billy Graham Association, there has emerged an international hegemony of evangelicals that effectively controls the flow of money, ideas, programs, and personnel on a global scale. Although persons of color are involved in the movement, it is clear that the control of this establishment is in the hands of North American whites. The established theology is Western, the establishment seminaries almost totally Anglo. This is especially true in schools of world mission.

It is for these reasons that minorities get nervous when they are exposed to another crusade to "let" the earth's people hear the gospel. The language of these crusades presupposes that a minority of the earth's population is the source of the church's evangelistic enterprise and that this minority is in control of the church's definitions of ministry and strategies of mission. This is true of finances. It is true of technology. It is true of politics. This establishment, like its secular model, is exclusive and, ironically, it is no less so by its attempt to be inclusive and international.[21]

The establishment has its ethical sensitivities sharpened by people from the two-thirds world and by dissidents within its own ranks in North America. Often denied access to the establishment press, these lower-caste sons of the pioneers have become a second sector within evangelicalism. They are tolerated by most of the establishment but grudgingly appreciated as well. Appreciated because they are the link to the people and issues that challenge the integrity of this global network.

This second sector among evangelicals represents the possibility that the establishment may rediscover a theology that defines the gospel in terms of reconciliation and justice. To discover this theology requires more than mere theological discourse. Some of us have come to this theology of reconciliation by way of the existential situation of living in a segregated society. Just as McGavran backed into homogeneous units in caste-bound India, we backed into a theology of reconciliation as victims of a racist society.

Why didn't this missionary giant associate the evils of caste with the evils of racism until recently? I think the answer has to do with the limitations of his theological horizons. One of the "rivers of thought" that influenced McGavran's life was the theological. "My pilgrimage was tremendously influenced both by the Eternal God's command and by the currents of theological opinions for and against biblical authority which have ebbed and flowed throughout the twentieth century," he explains. And what did he mean by biblical authority? The view of Scripture as the "inerrant revelation" of God's will for his church as that will manifested itself in Jesus Christ. To McGavran

> this is the only theological position which makes the communication of the Gospel, the discipling of *panta ta ethne* (all the peoples), the multiplication of congregations in every segment of mankind absolutely essential. This is the theological conviction which underlies the Church Growth movement.[22]

In his frame of reference, theology is reduced to a formula about the nature of Scripture. He is right about the relationship between an authoritative word and the church's obedience to that word in discipling the nations. But theology is concerned with more than merely a defense of the Bible as an inerrant text. Even a cursory reading of the Gospels conveys clearly the variety of responses to human need on the part of Jesus. The theology in Scripture is not just one theme, but many, all having a force and an authority. All are part of God's revelation of his attempt to make all things new, here and there, now and then. The outline is clear: Jesus intends nothing less than a new order, a new kingdom made up of new people, people reconciled to God and to each other.

For obvious reasons, reconciliation is central to the new order. You can't have "a kingdom of priests, a holy nation" if your followers are alienated, enemies in their minds, full of wicked works. Paul claims that this describes the human race and that God's antidote was reconciliation through the death of his son (Col. 1:21–22). Only through reconciliation with God can peace come (Eph. 2:13–18).

Note the overarching motif of reconciliation in the Colossians passage: not just mankind, but "all things, whether things on earth, or things in heaven."

Reconciliation and peace are linked in New Testament theology. God wills reconciliation and peace for a rebel race. Christ offers himself for that reconciliation. The final achievement of that becomes the passion of the Holy Spirit in whom both Jew and Gentile find access to God. That is the goal and the agenda of the triune God. The church's task is to take up that agenda.

Biblical theology is more than an exercise in determining the conditions under which disciples are best formed. Theology is more closely related to the *what* than the *how* of God's intentions for his creation. Of importance to the church's task today is the need to demonstrate that God's offer of salvation is good news to the oppressed and downtrodden. Johannes Verkuyl is right in asserting that "proclaiming the coming of the Kingdom is not enough. We are called to wait and to hasten toward the Kingdom of God in the awareness that neither waiting nor hastening is in vain—for we expect a new heaven and a new earth where justice will finally be at home."[23]

Our present, concrete history is shaped by politics. Richard Neuhaus puts it succinctly: ". . . politics is the chief enterprise to which we must attend in bringing about the changes we desire."[24] Yet this is not a new idea. To be sure, it rings with special meaning since the Enlightenment, and especially in America, where, as Henry May states, the Enlightenment is our religion.[25] But the Bible is about politics, about the relationship between politics and culture, and about the dynamics of religion as it operates at the core of culture. Thus the Bible is the church's basic political handbook. No one has seen this better than the late William Stringfellow who declared that

> . . . the biblical topic is politics. The Bible is about the politics of fallen creation and the politics of redemption; the politics of the nations, institutions, ideologies, and causes of this world and the politics of the Kingdom of God. The Bible expounds with extraordinary versatility, now one way and then another, and another, the singular issue of salvation— which is to say, the preemptive political issue.[26]

For many years theologians and councils have struggled with the relationship between the Scriptures and politics. Walter Rauschenbusch saw this relationship in the late 1800s and the social gospel movement was launched. It was one pastor's attempt to ask theology to address the grievous sores afflicting an urban people. The movement broke new ground in bringing a kingdom perspective to bear upon American society. It came apart because of its too naïve understanding of human nature and human societies. It simply is not possible to Christianize any social order nor is it the church's calling.

In the mid-sixties young theologians in the black church developed a decidedly political theology. James Cone in his early book *Black Theology, Black Power*, asserted that black power was Christ's central message to twentieth-century America. The National Conference of Black churchmen, in its famous "Black Power Statement" (1966), set the agenda for clergy and lay participation in numerous conferences "to differentiate true Christianity from white religion" as the only way forward toward solidarity with the oppressed.

The liberation motif arising out of the black church linked

with similar movements in Africa, Asia, and Latin America. Added to this was the strong influence of European scholars from Protestant and Roman Catholic roots with their theologies of hope. By the end of the 1970s a strong political theology spanning the globe was firmly in place.

But these theologies, while broadly ecumenical in their influence and similar in theme, had little effect upon the white church of North America. This was especially true of mainline evangelicals. What did influence these Christians was the political views of the World Council of Churches. No single group of Christians has struggled harder in recent years than the WCC to apply kingdom values to the political sphere. This pilgrimage may have climaxed at Bangkok in 1973 where the theme "Salvation Today" received a decidedly political interpretation. This was followed by the dramatic conclave in Nairobi in 1975 where kingdom themes were more carefully related to the church's missiological task. By the time the Council convened in Vancouver, British Columbia, in 1983, the themes of kingdom and evangelism had blended into a statement most objective evangelicals could applaud.

During this exciting if turbulent period in the Protestant church's struggle to find a theology for the times, the Roman Catholic Church produced a remarkable statement on evangelization. The Apostolic Exhortation of Pope Paul VI is thoroughly biblical and warmly evangelical. It is also political, part of the Vatican's attempt to undercut the impact of liberation theology among the churches in Latin America. Nevertheless, it is a powerful elucidation of the church's evangelistic task. It includes this statement:

> In the Church's mind, to evangelize means to bring the good news to every sphere of the human, so that its influence may work within mankind to transform it: "See I make all things new!" But the human race cannot be renewed unless individual men are first made new with the newness that flows from baptism and a life according to the Gospel. The aim of evangelization is to bring about this interior change. . . . The church evangelizes when she strives solely by the divine power of the message she proclaims, to

transform the hearts of each and every man, along with their activities, their lives and their whole environment.[27]

Aside from the sexist language, I am drawn to this statement and the following paragraph, which makes the definition more binding:

> We spoke of transforming every sphere of the human. The Church is not interested merely in preaching the Gospel in ever wider geographical areas and to ever larger multitudes of men. She wishes to touch and transform, by the Gospel's power, all the standards of judgment, the reigning values, the interests, the patterns of thinking, the motives, and ideals of mankind which are now in discord with God's word and his plan of salvation.[28]

In speaking of God's "plan of salvation," the Papal Exhortation identifies with Bangkok's emphasis upon "salvation today." This is the theme, the theological issue that requires the keenest attention. There simply will be no creative activity in the church, no authentic proclamation that "throbs with relevance to all conditions" of mankind, until our understanding of "salvation" is broadened. This is where the frontier in mission theology is staked out. This is where the biblical themes of incarnation and reconciliation are joined (2 Cor. 5:19); where justice and peace kiss each other (Ps. 85:10) and all things are made new (Rev. 21:5).

NOTES

[1]I've always liked J. B. Phillips' translation of vv. 15–16: "For he reconciled both to God by the sacrifice of one body on the cross, and by his act made utterly irrelevant the antagonism between them. Then he came and told both who were far off from God and us who were near, that the war was over."

[2]For instance, see Pat Robertson's argument in *Beyond Rationalism: How Miracles Can Change Your Life* (New York: Morrow, 1984).

[3]*U.S. News and World Report.*

[4] Saul Alinsky, "The Churches and Economic Structure," *Playboy.*

[5]William Julius Wilson, *The Declining Significance of Race, Blacks and Changing American Institutions,* 2d ed. (Chicago: Univ. of Chicago Press, 1980), 1–2.

[6]Christopher Lasch, *The Culture of Narcissism* (New York: Warner, 1979), 42.

[7]Elizabeth Drew, "A Political Journal," *The New Yorker* (October 29, 1984): 132.

[8]Daniel Yankelovitch, "New Rules in American Life," *Psychology Today* (April 1981): 36.

[9]Ibid., 40.

[10]A. R. Tippett, ed., *God, Man, and Church Growth* (Grand Rapids: Eerdmans, 1972), 171–72.

[11]Ibid.

[12]Ibid., 183.

[13]Slater, *The Pursuit of Loneliness,* 15.

[14]The point here is that issues such as justice will be mentioned in a given course. C. Peter Wagner, in answering his critics, wrote another text arguing that church growth is really committed to the "whole Gospel." But the fact that he had to write a separate book to argue this only highlights the point. Justice is not integral to the ideology of church growth.

[15]Theodore White, *America in Search of Itself: The Making of the President, 1956–1980* (New York: Harper and Row, 1982), 429.

[16]Slater, *The Pursuit of Loneliness,* 7.

[17]See the Lausanne Covenant in *Let the Earth Hear His Voice* (Minneapolis: Worldwide Publications, 1975), 4–5.

[18]Such as Houston '85, "Let Ethnics Hear His Voice," in which American blacks were excluded from significant participation. This

was done by defining ethnicity in terms of language rather than race (color). See also Stephen Knapp's critique of "post-Lausanne reflections" in *Partnership in Mission (May 1975)*.

[19]Leonard Silk and Mark Silk, *The American Establishment* (New York: Avon Discus, 1980), 16–17.

[20]C. Peter Wagner, who occupies the Chair of Church Growth at Fuller Seminary, School of World Mission, asserts that church growth is hermeneutically closer to psychology than it is to theology.

[21]For a helpful insight into the definitions and workings of the "establishment," see Leonard Silk and Mark Silk, *The American Establishment*.

[22]"That the Gospel Be Known," *Theology, News and Notes* (June 1985): 10–11.

[23]Johannes Verkuyl and H. G. Schulte Nordholt, *Responsible Revolution: Means and Ends for Transforming Society*, trans. Lewis Smedes (Grand Rapids, Eerdmans, 1974), 69.

[24]Richard John Neuhaus, *Time Toward Home: The American Experiment as Revelation* (New York: Seabury, 1975), 9, vii.

[25]Henry F. May, *The Enlightenment in America* (New York: Oxford Univ. Press, 1976), xiii.

[26]William Stringfellow, *An Ethic for Christians and Other Aliens in a Strange Land* (Grand Rapids: Eerdmans, 1973), 14–15.

[27]*Apostolic Exhortation*, ¶18.

[28]Ibid., ¶19.

3

The Second Conversion
of St. Peter

God is not obligated to ask permission of his people before he acts. Scripture makes this perfectly clear. Whether preparing to deliver his people from captivity in Egypt or engaging a woman at a well in Samaria, God seeks permission from no one. Luke captures this freedom of God in his fascinating account of the conversion of Cornelius (Acts 10). It is clear that God has set his heart upon this Gentile and that he intends to bless him in the same way he blessed the Jews: he will forgive his sins and fill him with the Holy Spirit and the assurance that he is accepted into the family of the saints. In so doing, Luke makes it clear that throughout this entire episode, God did not intend to seek permission from the Jewish believers in Jerusalem before he acted in Cornelius' behalf.

Dr. Luke has understood all along that salvation is God's work, and his alone. The sublime overtures made to Zechariah and Elizabeth, to Mary and Joseph indicate his sovereignty. The entire scheme of salvation, according to Luke, was orchestrated by God according to his divine counsel and foreknowledge (Acts 2:23; 4:28). It was God who set the eschatological calendar (Acts 1:7) and determined that all who believe in Jesus Christ would receive the promised Spirit (Acts 2:17). Furthermore, this is the same God who "made the heaven and the earth and the sea and everything in them" and who set the times of the earth's peoples, determining beforehand their places of habitation. He is at work among the peoples in order that they might seek him, reach out for him and find him (Acts 17:22–27).

Not only is God free to act without his people's permission, he is *free* to act. I suspect that the significance of the wind in Acts 1 is the same as in John 3. In both instances God declares his freedom in moving about the earth seeking those he has marked out for salvation. Though baffling and mysterious, he is constantly employing ways to set them up for the gospel.

Jesus knew this well. "My Father works hitherto," he said, "and so do I" (John 5:17). And a key activity of the Father was to draw people to the Son. All people (John 5:17–24; 6:44–51).

Luke's grasp of God's freedom to act is secure. He understands that the kingdom Jesus came to inaugurate is God's and not a revitalized Jewish state. He clearly sees it as open to all who put their trust in Jesus the Christ. Luke writes as an outsider, one who hears the Good News as if it were good news, or, as Robert McAffee Brown puts it, "unexpected news." Hence, he records its appeal to the sickly and the poor, the lame and the social outcasts. He carefully records the whole-souled embrace of the marginal people of society as a prominent feature of the ministry of Jesus and the early church. Someone had to care for these people. The empire wouldn't. The establishment religious leaders would not, choosing to walk by on the other side. Someone had to make room for these people, seek them out, let them know they were noticed, wanted, longed for and desired for their own sake.

The power of the Jesus movement lay in its ability to demonstrate a passionate commitment to the outcasts, the people at the margins of society. Of course, they *were* the society, for the most part. Marginality was especially true for women. Luke sees clearly that unless there is a place for women in the new order—something more than conducting prayer crusades and pouring tea—there would really be no movement at all. As it turned out, they would have the Spirit poured out upon them and they would prophesy.

In Luke's account of the early church in Acts, he is careful to record the work of the Spirit through both men and women. He mentions the work of Dorcas among the poor (Acts 9:36), and tells of God's pleasure when taking notice of the same work done by Cornelius. "God," said the angel to the centurion, "has heard your prayer and remembered your gifts to the poor" (Acts 10:31). This early historian is careful to record every evidence that the early church practiced the values of the kingdom as taught and practiced by Jesus during his earthly work. Luke's is a kingdom emphasis. He frames Acts at one end with Jesus speaking about the kingdom just prior to his ascension (1:3) and at the other end with Paul preaching the kingdom of God to all who came to see him in Rome (28:30–31).

There are numerous lessons crucial to the church's mission to be learned in Luke's account. We have already considered the matter of God's sovereignty. It includes his creativity and his lordship over the nations. He is in charge of the calendar of redemption, ordering all things according to his counsel and will. He may choose, indeed, has chosen, to reveal his will to the church, but he does not seek the permission of the church before he acts according to his own purposes for humankind.

Second, God is action-oriented. He is at work among the peoples of the earth in order to bring to fulfillment the prayer his Son taught the disciples to pray: that his name be hallowed, that his kingdom come, and that his will be done on earth. This is what God the Spirit is promoting and works both with and without the church to accomplish. But in working without the church's permission, or even the church's understanding, the Spirit does nothing contrary to the Word, so that the church, in moments of awareness, can trace the activity of God at any given time and discover his footsteps in the Scriptures. This happened in the Acts account as they sought to discover the significance of Cornelius' conversion (Acts 11:1–18).

Third, God listens carefully to the longings of devout men and women who, in their religious passions, seek to know him. They may be ill-informed or ignorant of him and his ways, but he listens and he acts in their behalf. God wants to be known by his creatures and has revealed himself in Jesus for this very reason.

Fourth, the kingdom message of the church was good news to most hearers. As Mark puts it in the opening of his gospel, "[This is] the beginning of the Gospel of Jesus Christ, the Son of God" (1:1). Furthermore, it is "the good news of God" (v. 14), and, as Jesus understands it, it is a gospel denoting the inbreaking of God's new order, the kingdom of God, and demands that all people repent of their sins as they enter. The good news is to be believed (v. 15). It is clear from all that follows in Mark's account that the common people heard Jesus gladly. What he said and what he did, his words and deeds, constituted good news to the masses.

Good news *must* be announced. John came into the wilderness preaching. Jesus began preaching immediately after his baptism. Their preaching demanded that men and women switch allegiance, convert to a new Master and Lord. The eyes of the people must be opened, and they must be turned from darkness to light, from the power of Satan to the power of God (Acts 26:18).

The Acts narrative is full of references to the preaching of the church. They proclaimed the Word of God everywhere. Their work was a rescue operation. When writing to the church at Colossae, Paul mentions this fact: "He has rescued us from the dominion of darkness and brought us into the kingdom of the Son he loves, in whom we have redemption, the forgiveness of sins' (1:13–14). Because this kingdom is God's, it follows that the earth's peoples must enter it on God's terms. They must repent and believe the gospel. Not all people repented on the same issues of course.

While the target of good preaching is the conscience of the hearers (2 Cor. 4:2) and the goal is conversion, no two people have the same experience of estrangement from God. Whole cultures vary greatly in their perceptions of what the gods require. But one thing is certain: a human race estranged from its Creator/Redeemer must be turned around, changed, reconciled. None are excepted. This is the real universalism: "All have sinned and fall short of the glory of God"; "there is no one righteous, not even one" (Rom. 3:23, 10). It follows that for this reason God gave his Son in order to redeem humankind from its sins. ". . . in Christ God was reconciling the world to himself" (2 Cor. 5:19, NRSV).

If sin and alienation are universal, salvation is both universal and particular. The gospel is about God's Son, Jesus Christ. God was in Christ reconciling the world unto himself. He was not in Buddha nor Abraham nor Paul or Peter. He is not in the church reconciling the world, although the church is obviously his agent for this task since the Resurrection. But the church did not die for the sins of the world as did Jesus, the Righteous One. He is the one who made expiation for the sins of the whole world (1 John 2:2). "In him we have redemption through his blood, the forgiveness of sins" (Col. 1:14). Ain't that good news!

Not everyone heard the announcement as good news; not everyone liked the messenger either, especially when they perceived that there was an amazing congruence between the word proclaimed and the one who proclaimed it. Religious figures, politicians, and other power brokers in society tended to be either amused or offended by it. Most of these people felt threatened by the obvious political implications of the movement among the masses. Christ's ministry was among the very people these leaders kept oppressing. This was intentional, and the oppressed people heard him with mounting joy. It works the same way today. One recalls the words of the late Rutilio Grande, the murdered priest of El Salvador. Speaking of the impact of the gospel upon the poor he observed that "for the campesinos [peasant farmers] the gospel was like light and air to men trapped all their lives in a mine shaft, and slowly they began to give up their magical ideas about religion."[1] While Jesus does not use the same term in his references to religion, it is clear that for most people in Palestine, religion functioned like magic in their lives. They were oppressed by their religion, unable to see through the mists of tradition and ritual kept alive by leaders who were themselves blind. Mere religion is never good news, especially to common people. The rich can always get around it for their own devices, but religion, like poverty, is always with the little people. What they need, and know that they need, is good news, a gospel that liberates.

A liberating gospel would need to be preached in the vernacular of the masses—no holy language, no esoteric, mystical incantation, no terminology shaped by a theological guild to provide access to the Word of God. This was the genius of the early evangelists, beginning with Jesus. The word spoken was understood by common people because it was couched in their own language. Language is at the core of a people's culture, at the heart of their self-understanding. Alter a people's language or force them to switch to someone else's, and you break continuity with their history, making their total world and lifeview obsolete. This has always been the object of invaders, whether the method was the blunt edge of the sword or the stiletto blade of economic colonialism. By preaching the gospel of the kingdom in the language of the common people, Jesus both validated their culture and at the same time relativized all claims of the culture to sovereignty over the people. This is seen throughout his ministry, and nowhere more tellingly than in his conversation with the woman in Samaria. It is clear that he had profound respect for this woman. While he was aware of the deficiencies of Samaritan religion, he nevertheless refused to convert her to Judaism as a prerequisite to finding God. His cross-cultural communication made it clear that neither Jew nor Gentile had either an advantage or a choice when coming to God; both would come to the Father on the same terms, "in spirit and in truth."

The emphasis in the Acts account is the same. Jesus Christ, risen from the dead, is Lord. Therefore, the nature gods were not, being exposed as mere superstitions and myths. The message was good news because it did not require a Gentile to become a Jew in order to be set free from sin; it was all right for one to be a Gentile in any culture since God was comfortable in any culture, celebrating its worth and values as long as they were not a focus of idolatry. It has always been easy to get Jesus to come to dinner; it has not been so easy to turn over the keys to the house to him.

Thus, it came as a terrible shock to both Gentile and Jew when the story of God's dealing with Cornelius came to light. Cornelius had the same need for forgiveness as did the Jews of Jerusalem, only for different reasons. If the Jews were guilty of the blood of Christ, their Messiah, Cornelius was anguished because he had no assurance that his sins were forgiven in spite of years of faithful praying, giving, and serving.

Cornelius needed more than assurance of forgiveness before God. One senses in the Acts account that he also sought acceptance within a community of people who knew God. He yearned to belong to a people who belonged to God. This is the underside of the doctrine of alienation. It is the feeling side of it, the reality of alienation where one knows that to be whole one must be in community; that to be reconciled to God is only part of the restoration. Thus the church becomes in God's plan the new humanity in Christ.

More than a doctrine, a slogan waving over some deeper life conference, or some mystical union celebrated by the saints as a badge of their orthodoxy, union with Christ is to be a practical, palpable relationship with others in the same body. Cornelius knows this even if he does not know that he knows it. The yearning to belong is as fundamental as the need to belong. Wholeness comes about in the merger of the two: to be is to belong to someone.

The unanswered questions were out there: will God accept Cornelius, a non-Jew? Was there anyone out there who, speaking for God, would be a part of his new life should he convert? There *was* someone out there who spoke for God. There always is. God is never without a witness—not for long anyhow. Peter spoke the word of God, Cornelius and his household believed, and God gave these Gentiles the witness of the Spirit as a sign and seal of their acceptance. He forgave their sins and flooded their joy-filled hearts with peace.

But the church had greater difficulty answering the second question. There isn't always somebody out there ready to accept someone who is not their kind. Without that someone the process toward salvation is not complete. This was a crucial point God set Peter up to learn. It came into fuller view through the vision God gave to Paul. And it became central to the Pauline teaching of the work of the Cross in breaking down all the barriers between humankind and God and among the tribes of the earth.

Luke is careful to record how the church, including Peter,

struggled with the follow-up program. The issue was not technique but principle. The puzzle concerned God's intentions in sending Peter to Caesarea. If it was to save a pagan—well, that was one thing, perhaps a good thing. After all, those people need saving. But if there was something more . . . It is here that Luke seems to glow with that inner light of the historian who has begun to see the point of the story out of the reams of material at his disposal. Luke clearly sees that God is forming a new society in the earth, a new humanity among the peoples of the earth.

Thus the significance of Cornelius in Luke's account. He represents another phase in the unfolding of God's eternal purpose in human history. Though this devout Gentile was a flesh-and-blood human, he was also a symbol to the church of God's salvific history, a people who will be an object lesson to principalities and powers of God's many-faceted wisdom (Eph. 3:10).

The church in Jerusalem knew some of this. They knew that God was sovereign Lord of the nations (Acts 4). They preached a kingdom message offering forgiveness of sins to those who repented and believed in Jesus. They were committed to evangelism and filled Jerusalem with the word of God. They demonstrated their commitment to the new order by sharing their possessions and goods. They genuinely loved one another. But it apparently had not dawned upon them that God's new humanity included Gentiles as fellow heirs.

The church could be excused for this since even Paul confessed that this dimension of the divine purpose had been "hidden to past generations" and was only now revealed to him (Eph. 3:2–6, PHILLIPS). It is possible, however, that the early leaders did not see this divine plan because of a too-selective reading of the Scriptures. If read from a particular cultural preference, Scripture can be made to support rather narrow and parochial interests. Thus James can understand God's purpose for the Gentiles only after the event in Cornelius' house. The teaching had been there all along however (Acts 15:13–18; Amos 9:11–12). That teaching was simply that God would bring salvation to the Gentiles through Israel—a radical idea, yet one calculated to reinforce a sense of specialness in a chauvinist. The new revelation was that God would unite Jew and Gentile as partners in salvation, thus creating a new humanity. That would take some getting used to. But it was good news!

Peter is an example of a certain kind of evangelical blindness. He is loved the world over for his bumbling orthodoxy, his passionate devotion to Christ, and his need to be converted every once in a while. He is the apostle of conversion. One could almost build the case that when Jesus commanded him to strengthen the brothers once he was converted (Luke 22:32) that he had outlined Peter's life calling. But that view is scarcely the whole story with the man. Luke records his ministry as a seasoned bishop of the church. He is in full possession of his apostolic gifts and exercises his authority to bring much health and growth to the church (Acts 3–5, 10–12). He is a gifted preacher and respected leader in the Jerusalem assembly. Yet he needs to be converted.

The Jerusalem church, like Peter, for all its significance as the mother church—Old First Church—needs converting as well. It's not because sin runs rampant among its members. Nothing so dramatic. The church needs converting because God is doing a work so radical that unless they change they cannot fully share in it. God is not seeking the permission of the church for this new venture; he is not waiting on the church to "pray it down." What he is doing is demonstrating his intentions with a view to persuading the saints to get on board. In order to get the Jerusalem church committed to the new agenda, the Spirit seeks out one of its leading elders and begins a work of conversion in him. The apostle Peter converted once again.

What *are* God's intentions? God intends to effect reconciliation across the vast reaches of the cosmos, to ensure that in the culmination of human history, when the times will have reached their fulfillment, all things in heaven and earth will be brought together under the headship of Jesus Christ (cf. Eph. 1:9–10; Col. 1:19–20). For this reason, the ministry of the church is always a ministry of reconciliation (2 Cor. 5:16–21). It

71

is imperative that the church discover why in our day we are not making this a dominant value in evangelism.

Luke helps us by his account. For one thing, it is clear that Peter sees the Jews, including the believers among whom he labors, as special in the sight of God. He considers it an unlawful thing for a Jew to associate with or to visit anyone of another nation (Acts 10:28). The reference is probably to any kind of social intercourse, anything that, in the normal course of human affairs, might lead to contamination of religion, personal or group ethics, or cultural values. Of course God did require that his people be separate from other nations. They were to be a people for his own possession and they were to demonstrate this allegiance by keeping free from rival loyalties. But the purpose in all this was that once God had secured a special people, he would reveal himself through them to the nations.

Like many nations afflicted with a sense of specialness, the Jews confused grace with merit and substituted all manner of regulations to reinforce their sense of uniqueness, blending their legalism with an intense form of nationalism. By the time Peter falls heir to the cultural legacy, it bears little resemblance to the divine calling: a royal priesthood, a holy nation, a chosen people declaring God's praise. Sadly, the best they could offer to the nations was toleration to the few godfearers who ventured into the synagogue, or, in the case of Jewish believers, to justify separation from Gentiles by the lame remark that it is unlawful to socialize with you folks.

Peter and his generation had succumbed to the deception of a misunderstood chosenness. The tradition, that they were a special people in God's sight, contained enough truth, enough verifiable history, to make it most attractive. But it was mixed with enough error to make it dangerous. At the extreme end of such a cultural perspective is the ideology of racism and, with it, a thousand oppressions leveled against those on the outside of the culture as well as against those on the inside who might disagree with the ruling elite.

Such a malady is caused by the notion that the gods, or in Israel's case, Jehovah, has chosen a people by virtue of some intrinsic and superior quality that commends them to that god. Such a notion completely vitiates the grace of God in freely choosing any people for himself. Out of this mentality emerges a corporate messianism, a conviction that such a culture is destined to rule the world—or at least that part of the world within its reach. It was because of the injustice caused by such a distorted national self-understanding that the prophets were sent to Israel. (See especially Amos 7:14–17. They charged repeatedly that Israel's sin was to have forgotten God and become idolaters. The form of their idolatry included national-ism accompanied by jingoistic rituals. The classic illustration of this is found in the language and lamentations of Isaiah and Jeremiah, and reveals the devastation that can come to a people when religion is corrupted to serve nationalistic ends.

Nationalism is a basic human expression of a people's awareness of itself as a people. However, since the end of World War II nationalism has become a global reality to be reckoned with. With the development of the cold war, new terms came into existence to define the new alliances that were taking place, or that Western leaders hoped would take place. Thus such terms as "first world," "second world," and "third world" came into being. Each term defines not simply a geopolitical reality, but also a way of dividing up the world according to economic systems and economic power. As country after country reclaimed its ancient identity, political movements sprang up to give further definition to a new age— national liberation fronts from Africa to South Vietnam to Greece. Currently, the most famous such movement is the Palestine Liberation Organization. Even within the borders of the United States in the 1960s an abortive attempt at revolution was termed the Symbionese Liberation Movement.

Timothy Smith asserts that "nationalism is by no means the only or most important force at work in contemporary politics or society. But in recent history, nationalism as a movement and ideology has become increasingly prevalent and perhaps dominant, even over communism."[2]

In recent history, in Hitler's Germany, Khomeni's Iran, Begin's Israel, Botha's South Africa, and in Reagan's America, it is difficult to imagine these movements toward nationalism apart from a resurgent religious fundamentalism. They are there, each with some well-chosen name—The Moral Majority, ultra-Orthodox Jews, Protestantism and Roman Catholicism in Northern Ireland, al-Fatah in Palestine. Speaking of the latter movement Sami Hadawi has said that their principles were no different from those of any other liberation movement, including that of the American Revolution. The purpose was "to remove the evils and injustices imposed upon them and to regain their *God-given* [italics mine] right of freedom and security to which they are fully entitled."[3] These groups often exist to validate various forms of political and cultural chauvinisms, "rights," if you will. Furthermore, they may have their strongest claim on a nation at those precise moments when the political glue within the society seems to have lost its strength—when the political establishment seems weak and unable to win the allegiance of its constituencies. For communities of true believers, such a time presents a theological question that must be asked: does God belong to our tribe? Is he the author of our political ideology? Does he baptize our interpretation of history, our pretensions to dominance, even in the name of compassion and freedom?

It may seem to be stretching to make the connection between Peter's theological chauvinism and the current forms of nationalism. But Peter's theology and his nationalism were intertwined in ways of which he was not aware. His problem was a form of nationalism that penetrated to the core of his being, and being Spirit-filled did not eradicate this other spirit from his heart. Some would argue that the Spirit would not take his Jewishness from him, but Jewishness is not the same thing as nationalism, except perhaps among fundamentalists. National pride, what Americans call patriotism, dies hard in most believers—especially if one is convinced intellectually, theologically, and culturally that God is the author and exclusive promoter of one's national existence. This one issue, although not the only one facing the church, is the key to its integrity and evangelistic credibility as we enter the next century.

The issue of national pride among believers is further complicated by a need always to contextualize the gospel. The church at Jerusalem had seen the Spirit respond to the need of various people to encounter the gospel in a way that each could understand. The church was a Jewish church at its core. But Pentecost was more than a Jewish event. The gospel was heard in many languages representing many nations. Babel was being reversed and a new "language" united new believers from many nations. A new unity of a different sort was being fashioned in the earth. It would be based not upon national origin, but upon life in the Spirit.

This original unity, which was witnessed at Pentecost, seems to have been lost or ignored by much of the church's leadership, including Peter. The Jerusalem church became Jewish and nobody seemed to be bothered by it. The breakthrough came at Antioch, where, for perhaps the first time, the Spirit persuaded the saints to get the whole view of the gospel (Acts 13). No one understood this need for contextualization better than Paul. Yet he is the foremost proponent of the doctrine of reconciliation, the unifying theme of his theology.

Addressing the theme of mission in the 1980s, Lesslie Newbigin identified the issue of contextualization as the key to its call. But then in an unexpected twist, he focused the issue on Western churches. Aware of the efforts of Western missiologists to confront the challenges posed by cultural contexts beyond their borders, the noted missionary/scholar contended that similar efforts must be made to understand identical challenges at home, i.e., in the West.

> Yet it is the West that ought to be giving missiologists their most worrying questions. It is in the West that the church appears to be continuously losing ground. It is typically the product of Western enlightened culture to whom the good news appears irrelevant nonsense. Yet one does not find (at least in my limited reading) that missiologists are giving the same intense and sustained attention to the problems of finding the "dynamic equivalent" for the Gospel in Western society as they are giving to that problem as it occurs in the meeting with peoples of the Third World.[4]

This is an extremely important insight. The reasons for this oversight are many, but at the root of it is a historic unwillingness in the West to apply the Cross to its reigning ideology of white supremacy. This is one of the main reasons the threat of syncretism, so feared by Western missiologists when viewing their task in the third world, is overlooked when viewing the same task at home. Western leaders fear syncretism abroad— the dreaded admixture of gospel with the more "pagan" aspects of culture—so detrimental to Christian life. But there is an equally detrimental effect of modern paganisms in the West upon the Christian church.

White racism is one of those paganisms. God is not a white male and Western civilization is not a secular equivalent of the kingdom of God. To argue this again is to flirt with a cliché. Samuel Escobar, as long ago as the 1974 Lausanne Conference, labeled this mentality "culture Christianity," and implied that it was the chief export of North American missions.

Evangelicals continue to hold conferences on evangelism and are in the process of passing the torch to a new generation of "emerging" leaders. But unless they face up to their own captivity to Western paganisms, they are likely to pass on more than the gospel. Or their efforts will be summarily dismissed by emerging leaders who have long ago transcended an earlier fascination with a tired Western leadership still chained to its unsavory past. Peter was to learn that God wasn't Jewish and that Jerusalem was not his sole dwelling place. Such lessons would come hard, and nothing short of conversion at a deep level would accomplish God's purpose for a new day of mission outreach.

The second conversion of St. Peter happened in a manner appropriate for any person professing loyalty to Jesus Christ. His experience had both a vertical and a horizontal dimension. As the story is recorded in Acts 10, Peter sees a vision from God (the vertical) and hears voices from the street (the horizontal). In both instances it is God whose voice is being heard. Specific guidance is likely to be discerned where those two sources of light intersect. The timing is perfect; the voices—from above and from the streets—unmistakable. The apostle of conversion is now set up for another conversion experience.

The Western church is set up to experience a similar conversion if only it can be helped to hear what God is saying. Currently it is divided between two capacities, capacities and abilities that are not evenly distributed among all the parts of the church. One might say that it is of two minds or of two spirits.

One part of the church claims the ability to hear the Word of the Lord, to fathom its mysteries, to comprehend immediately any visions from on high. This tradition inclines toward mysticism, miracles, immediate communication with God, and it attempts to get beyond rationalisms to a direct perception of what God is doing in the world. Some elements of this tradition are free to borrow from the social sciences and argue passionately that without some such dependence on human knowledge and expertise, there is no way the gospel can be freed from cultural captivities. But this segment of the church still claims to get its guidance directly from on high. Thus the current attraction of the charismatic experience and the appeal of signs and wonders.

Curiously, this group is suspicious of voices from the street. It does, however, show signs of being captive to voices from academic halls. Anthropology is fine in the service of the gospel, but when the little people cry out for liberation, all sorts of flags go up among this segment for fear that the gospel will be lost in such a secular pursuit. Yet the gospel has been obscured in most of the cultural trappings of the Enlightenment for many years, trappings that have always favored the rich and powerful.

This ability to discern the ways of the Lord by visions and voices from above translates into all sorts of wondrous techniques and not a little passion. And what slogans! The banners! The international convocations! These are they who let the peoples of the earth hear the voice they have heard. Or think they have heard. Well and good. But Luke says Cornelius has already heard his voice. Not clearly enough to be saved say some of the Jews, but the same voice nonetheless. God has shown that he is already on the case long before his people even know there is a case. Cornelius is a marked man, just as surely as the gazelle-like Dorcas had been in Acts 9. Angels had been dispatched to Cornelius' house, one at least, and probably one who had considerable experience in carrying God's word to Israel in other days. God clearly intends to save this man and his household. A piece of cake.

To convert Peter and the church takes a bit more doing. The difficulty of this is as understandable in North America today as at Caesarea long ago. Lacking a strong tradition—one that would offer guidance and direction in these matters— modern evangelicals have to rely upon other means by which to discern God's will. Thus, they have come to depend upon personalities and upon taking the right side on debatable issues. Battles become necessary at frequent intervals in order to insure that purity be maintained. Distance from other believers who do not line up with the prevailing definitions is as important as keeping oneself unspotted from the world. The spectacle of a television evangelist who was exposed for his sexual sins telling his denomination to take a hike is a graphic example of the dominance of personality and warfare in evangelical circles.

So in the current fascination with signs and wonders one segment of the church has staked out its manner of "hearing God" and discerning his will. While much of this current emphasis has been forgotten by most of the church, it has been one part of the church's heritage for centuries. Today, however, there are some new twists. The power and authority of this movement are largely in the hands of individuals or independent organizations whose willingness to submit to the church's councils is questionable.

Another part of the church boasts of its ability to discern the will of God by listening to "voices from the street." Indeed its practice of taking the people on the streets seriously is one way this segment of Christians defines itself and argues for its orthodoxy. Their ears are tuned to the world, not the church. Until recently, these believers have asserted that the streets set the agenda for the church: "Hear these voices, feel this pulse, and you'll know where God is." It is in the street, in the voices of people yearning for fullfilment and freedom, that one hears the Voice. The mystical experience with the One From Above, as a separate encounter, is not really needed.

These believers also have conferences. And banners! And slogans! They even have women leading their meetings and articulating their theology! In the first century this group would have gone to Cornelius' house and announced the good news that he was already "saved" because he had been an anonymous Christian all along. They would have cited as evidence his concern for the poor and his ecumenical outreach to the Jewish community.

Admittedly, I have indulged in overstating the posture and behavior of each of these segments in the church. The encouraging reality is that neither of these groups is the same today. The World Council of Churches has moved more in the direction of the Word of God and evangelism, though practice still lags behind pronouncement. At the same time, evangelicals have moved in the direction of social involvement, seeking to be more sensitive to the voices from the street. So much so, in fact, that some of the establishment leaders feel called upon to reissue the warning against too much listening to or dialogue with the other lest evangelism be blunted or compromised. Further to insure against this possibility, their platforms are carefully guarded lest some Philistine in Israel rally the troops.

In reality, there is as much lag in a consistent evangelical practice of social ethics as there is in a consistent demonstration of the WCC's commitment to evangelism. But there is movement among both groups.

The impetus for change among both of these segments has been supplied by evangelicals from the two-thirds world. Westerners—liberal and conservative—and their liberal counterparts in the rest of the world have been forced to listen to the voices from the street and to acknowledge that God has cleansed these people as he has also cleansed us. Furthermore, the cleansing was the work of the same Holy Spirit who changed our lives. The evidence for this is the shift in Christian population from the West to the non-West, especially Africa and the Far East. While Westerners have been redemptively involved in some of this growth, fast-growing churches have spawned new movements in evangelism that have far-reaching implications for the future of the entire Christian enterprise. The impact of this on conciliar and non-conciliar missiology is the subject of much discussion in all Western circles.

Perhaps no other issue exposes American evangelical chauvinism more than the near total absence of African-American participation in these discussions at the very time that Western influence is up for grabs in much of the non-West. The lockout is not total. There are several individuals who are recognized dutifully by the leadership of the movement. They are usually employed on platforms during plenary sessions. They are often not the ones engaged in serious discussion. Other prominent African-American evangelicals who are not invited are often perceived to have an agenda the old guard finds objectionable. Meanwhile, leaders from the two-thirds world are beginning to raise questions about the absence of these brothers from America. Unfortunately, the answers to their queries are often supplied by the very people responsible for keeping African-Americans out.

It seems that evangelical mission leaders are still wary of people of color in their midst. Perhaps, as the people of color have opportunity to hear the Voice from above and the Voice from below, they might be reminded of their cultural captivity at home. Ironically, any sensitivity Anglo evangelicals have toward captive people derives more from the influence of the black civil rights movement than evangelical Protestant theology.

There is still another irony. Some black thinkers suspect that white leadership fears that the agenda they (the white leadership) outline would be undermined by enlarging the participation. Is it possible, they wonder, that the spirit of Martin Luther King, Jr., may have captured the hearts and minds of leaders trained in evangelical schools, rendering them unworthy to participate as members of the club. They wouldn't be "qualified" to take upon themselves leadership of the evangelical movement because they would come to the task by a different path. This fear has its counterpart overseas where one can see an attempt by some evangelicals to keep third world leaders away from some North American black leaders. The concern is that these third world church leaders could also be too sympathetic to the influence of King. For to many people of color the world over, King was a major leader of Christianity in the West, and they are only now learning that Western missiologists in the evangelical camp have yet to take him seriously. (The point here is not that King was a missiologist or an evangelical. The issue is one of control and who claims the right to define and judge the issues.)

Some members of the worldwide evangelical movement, notably from Europe, seem put off by the African-American style of debate. It may not be sufficiently Oxfordian in its manners. Perhaps it is too emotional, more like Latino discussions. "But of course," the argument goes, "we do include blacks in our conferences and other gatherings." When it is pointed out that they are small group and devotional leaders, the response is, "We try to find the best, most capable people we can for these conferences." The remark is chauvinist at best. At worst, it is blatantly racist. Our European brothers need a copy of the infamous television remarks by the late and unlamented executive of the Los Angeles Dodgers. To argue that it is difficult to find capable black thinkers for conferences where crucial issues in the mission of the church are decided is tantamount to saying that black people cannot be found for "thinking" positions in American sports because of certain genetic deficiencies. Somebody needs converting; someone needs to call another Jerusalem conference.

The Western church is divided and it is of no comfort to observe that non-Western churches are also. It is divided along racial lines, not "ethnic," that marvelously useful term that can mask all sorts of attitudes that in earlier days would have been labeled racialist. The evangelical church is further divided along class lines, divisions created not only by economics, but also by differing definitions of what Christian ministry ought to be. To be sure, economic standing is significant and is often determinative of the latter.

81

The evangelical class divisions are based upon commitments and priorities. There is, for instance, a first class that champions evangelism and church growth at the expense of social responsibility. Then comes a second class whose attempts to champion a marriage between evangelism and social ethics has them branded as mere social activists. (Among the conciliar churches there is a first class that majors on the church's social responsibility at the expense of evangelistic activity and a second class that desires passionately to do responsible evangelism as well as to continue the great tradition of social activism practiced in the decades between 1960 and 1980.)

But such class distinctions are also the product of ideological differences, and we all subscribe to one or more of them. "Let him who is without ideology cast the first stone." These ideologies affect definitions of ministry as surely as do other hermeneutical constructs. They are expressions of worldviews that, because they are pre-evangelistic, determine the way in which evangelism and mission are viewed—or skewed.

This is not to downplay the significance of class distinctions based on economics. Those Westerners who make most of the distinctions and apply them to strategies for ministry are affluent. By virtue of their positions in academic institutions or para-church organizations, they constitute an elite. They are not wealthy themselves, but they have access to those who are, or to those who have created organizations and foundations whose support is critical for the purposes decided upon by these elites. The price of such support is usually the assurance that the goals of the elites do not conflict with the reigning political or economic ideology of the foundation or supporting institution. The agenda, precisely because it is controlled by this elite, tends toward the reigning ideology of the sponsor. Or put another way, the agenda, because it must not offend the sponsor's ideologically inspired values, gets shaped by the elite in such a way as to insure that the practice of ministry does not raise serious questions about those values.

Even curricula in seminaries and schools of mission are affected by the interplay of ideology, wealth, and elitist power. Anyone called upon to address the issue of liberation, for instance, had better do it in a "responsible manner," which means in such a way that donors or constituents do not get the impression that the professor really advocates that as part of the gospel. Thus, not only are definitions of ministry at stake, but also the deeper understanding of the gospel itself, to say nothing of academic freedom and integrity of the institution.

The interplay of ideology with wealth and power are key issues as the church heads into the next century. With the internationalization of the theological enterprise in sight, definitions are going to be severely scrutinized both in terms of content and place of origin. The advice of the famous Watergate informant to "follow the money" in pursuit of the culprits will be rechristened to read, "follow the definitions," for they who make the definitions control the mission. At the end of the century there will be serious attempts to pass the baton to future leaders.

Westerners, in spite of past mistakes, are busily engaged in finding leaders, especially in the colored world, to whom they can hand over the baton (or, more accurately, share it). But baton-passing is a delicate maneuver. (I can only imagine with what delicacy one would pass a torch!) It requires timing, rhythm, and much practice. Signals have to be arranged, strides measured. It is not enough simply to state as a matter of fact that all who run in the race are on the same team. There are subtle distinctions.

If relationships among believers, i.e., reconciliation, is the central issue in the church's agenda, then the metaphor of baton-passing may be inappropriate. No single metaphor can bear the weight of all the truth a word rich in meaning intends to convey. The central problem with the passing of the baton lies in the fact that a baton is not passed until the one holding it is ready to give it to the person designated to receive it. This would mean, in ecclesiastical politics, that a younger generation, or the new people on the block, whether younger or not, would need to wait until the previous generation decided it was time to pass on the heritage. In an entrepreneurial society such as ours, batons don't get passed anyhow. They get snatched. Or a new generation simply buys a new track and sets up another competition, provided, of course, that they get a good contract from a sponsor. In such a culture the issue is not what's what, or even who's who, but who's hot and who's not. There is no thought of reconciliation in this kind of world.

The situation among leaders in the evangelism industry today is not unlike the relationship of the disciples to Jesus. He had recruited his people. They were called to be with him and to practice a ministry that he would define and pass on to them. Communion, learning, and obedience—this was the agenda. They had consented to be his followers, and they did so with enthusiasm. But, to be honest, the quality of their relationships was often embarrassing. Yet they had some semblance of an excuse. They had no idea of the standard to which they must conform, at the outset at least.

It took the disciples a while to realize that their priority was to become a new people, a new humanity. What they were to be had to overshadow what they were to do. Indeed, what they did in his name would be validated or questioned on the basis of their behavior. These disparate people from different regions and walks of life in a tiny, no-account country had to become brothers and sisters. They had to surrender their passions for power and learn to wash one another's feet. Their personal ambitions had to be reigned in and subordinated to something larger. They learned to celebrate the new ambition that was constrained by being in the service of Jesus Christ. But they were not to behave as if answering the call to follow Jesus put them into an exclusive society. They needed to hear him say that "he who is not against us is for us," and that "others have labored and you have entered into their labors."

Passing the baton, for Jesus, had to do with dying. Without the cross there would be no baton. Thus the cross became the centerpiece of the movement, the symbol that change, however passionately desired, would always prove costly. Old habits, old ways of thinking long associated with the old guard, had to be subjected to the light of Scripture and courageous leadership. People, long-distanced from the family of God by ancient prejudices, had to be brought close for fellowship and mutual edification and instruction. Jerusalem had to deal with the good news coming out of Caesarea and beyond, even to Antioch. New partnerships had to be developed and new gifts assessed in the light of the Spirit's leading.

As is often the case when new breakthroughs in human relations are called for, the Holy Spirit seeks and finds new people to blaze the trail. They are not always the "names" in the movement. Today we are in desperate need of new Barnabases, for there are many Pauls out there whose hearts the Lord has already touched but whose reputation is a bit chancy for establishment types. They must be found and brought into the larger family of the church. They must also be followed. But before that can happen the church's leadership must learn to discern the voice of the Spirit concerning them. There are many such people in the family worldwide. They are being recognized as leaders in their own contexts and have much to contribute to the rest of us. We must develop ears with which to hear what the Spirit is saying to us through them.

What is also needed is a willingness to acknowledge their value as colleagues anywhere in the world. They too are world Christians. Our brothers and sisters in the two-thirds world have seen God use them in spearheading incredible growth. Furthermore, they have a far more developed and robust spirituality than we know. This is critical because the issue confronting the church is not the growth of churches numerically, but the integrity of the churches as a demonstration of the gospel's power to forge a new humanity in the earth. Integrity does not oppose growth. The two are closely related. But currently the question before the house is not whether we have the technique to grow churches. It is whether the ones we grow amount to much in terms of godly character, whether they are signs of the new order or not.

Whether or not the church in the West makes reconciliation a central element in evangelism is terribly important. But it is not so critical that it can thwart what God is going to do in the world. The Holy Spirit, when he was prevented from doing a complete work in the church of Jerusalem, simply went up the road to Antioch. God can get along nicely without the Western churches—witness the vitality of God's people in China in spite of its being "closed." The church is important anywhere, but the nagging question today is whether the church in the West has become as redundant as other Western institutions precisely at the moment when a new partnership in mission is most promising.

If the gospel was good news because it produced a new humanity in the earth, forging new partnerships in mission, it was also good news because it brought a living God into the world of politics, economics, religion, art, and the games. He was revealed as a God, not of austere mein, full of holiness and laden with laws and innumerable ordinances with which to inflict a helpless race. Nor was he a deity aloof and unconcerned about oppression, militarism, and greed. The God of good news wore the face of Jesus, and later the face of Paul, Priscilla, Peter, and Dorcas. He had clothed himself in human flesh once and radically changed history. The good news was that he is still active in history, calling those in whom he lives to make a difference in their immediate locale. There was to be no more standing on the sidelines. No more toleration of a private, mystical religion and a public faith in gods who were no gods. The gospel of the kingdom called men and women from the grandstand and forced them to play the game.

This contribution of the early Christians was a major breakthrough in the history of relationships between sects and their culture. Historically, a religious sect saw itself as an integral part of culture and its gods were inextricably bound to that culture, as often as not legitimating it. It was expected that the gods would take care of the society's needs and in return the society would offer up its sacrifices in allegiance to the gods. In Greco-Roman times this whole affair was largely ceremonial. The citizenry would observe the nationalistic rituals when the politicians called upon them to do so, but there was little connection between what we would call private faith and public behavior.

Roman civilization provides a paradigm for grasping the impact of the gospel on a given culture. Rome was an urban culture. The Christians at Rome were urban believers. Rome was a polyglot culture and would be called a world-class city in the jargon of today's missiological enterprise. J. P. V. D. Balsdon asserts that Rome's population at the end of the Republic and the beginning of the Empire was between three quarters of a million and a million persons. Of this number, approximately 200,000 to 250,000 were slaves.[5] The city was cosmopolitan—peasants from the countryside, foreigners from Egypt to India, and resident Romans. By 44 B.C. it was estimated that three fourths of the population was composed of people of foreign ancestry.

Romans were a proud people. They were fiercely nationalistic, and due to their string of military conquests had come to think of themselves as a unique race. The gods had smiled upon them and theirs was a god-blessed society. Balsdon again offers perspective:

> Roman success was proof enough of her enjoyment of divine favor. In a letter to the island of Teos in 193 B.C. it was stated that "our piety is evident from favor of the gods which we enjoy." The Romans were the god's own people, in fact. Romans were the master race, *populus victor gentium*.[6]

The Romans were as snobbish and arrogant as they were successful in combat. Their wars were just wars, and even their infrequent defeats were exemplary of Roman virtues of courage in the face of overwhelming numbers. To the Romans, the Greeks were effete, dainty, prissy, and in matters of combat gutless. Greeks were playboys, fascinated with words, and pretty words at that. To the Greeks, Romans were simply barbaric. The Greek divided the world into two classes— Greeks and barbarians. The apostle to the Gentiles was to assert that the gospel had made him a debtor to both.

There are parallels between Roman culture and that of the West in our time: fascination with power, urban culture with cities becoming more and more polyglot, the influence of abundance upon the values and morality of the host society, wealth derived from the plunder of other nations, the myth-making of historians and politicians to justify armed aggression, and the vision of the dominant culture as god-blessed and anointed. This vision is a version of master-race ideology married to religion.

Richard Sennett sees one other important parallel: Both cultures in a period of decline failed to balance public and private life. Sennett sees Roman public life after Augustus as largely a formality, civic duties seen largely as duties with little or no passion "in . . . acts of conformity." He goes on to say,

> As the Roman's public life became bloodless, he sought in private a new focus for his emotional . . . energies . . . new principles of commitment and belief. This private commitment was mystic, concerned with escaping the world at large and the formalities of the *res publica* as part of that world. This commitment was to various near Eastern sects, of which Christianity gradually became dominant; eventually Christianity ceased to be a spiritual commitment practised in secret, burst into the world, and became itself a new principle of public order.[7]

The last phrase is crucial. That which began as a small sect offering allegiance to some strange deity gradually became a "new principle of public order." This seems inevitable given both the nature of Greco-Roman government and the nature of the relationship God sustains with both history and his people, not only in the private realm where individuals interact one on one, but also in the public realm where the "powers" pretend to deserve the absolute loyalty of all citizens. The gospel exposed those pretensions and set people free to be responsible for their lives, their relationships, and their society. If Jesus was Lord, Caesar was not.

Roman formalism has its modern counterpart. Westerners seem, for the most part, to be casual in their public duties. They will vote for their vested interests, usually economic, and rise to the occasion for the brief emotional excretion of patriotic sentiment. In human relations we tend to be formal, especially toward strangers and especially when these strangers are encountered in cities. When confronted with institutional structures beyond family or neighborhood, the *res publica*, citizens in the West go along without much investment in either passion or commitment. The exception would seem to be the new right, defined either by political ideology or theological commitment. But this exception is mere illusion. Much of the movement is made up of people who are being asked to send money. For the most part that is what the constituency is doing. There is an occasional march against abortion, a demonstration for prayer in the schools, a bumper sticker pledging support for some conservative candidate, or a knot gathered in front of a porno shop.

But there is a distinction to be made between the Roman culture in decline and Western cultural in decline. Says Sennett,

> The difference between the Roman past and the modern present lies in the alternative, in what privacy means. The Roman in private sought another principle to set against the public, a principle based on religious transcendence of the world. In private, we seek not a principle, but a reflection, that of what our psyches are, what is authentic in our feelings. We have tried to make the fact of being in private, alone with ourselves and with family and intimate friends, an end in itself.[8]

The shift Sennett describes is a subtle one, but crucial to the evangelizing mandate of the church. What is being described is a retreat from public passion to a private preoccupation with cultural feelings, the pursuit of aloneness as an end in itself. Or, if you will, the privatization of the social. This sounds like the famous point argued by Tocqueville in his celebrated definition of individualism. The famed French cultural analyst had this to say:

> Individualism is a calm and considered feeling which disposes each citizen to isolate himself from the mass of his fellows and withdraw into the circle of family and friends; with this little society formed to his taste, he gladly leaves the greater society to look after itself.[9]

Today, a century later, this same individualism translates into what amounts to a therapeutic society where even one's civic commitments and family ties are viewed as adjuncts to personal wholeness or self-fulfillment. In a fine and penetrating commentary on the relationship between independent individualism and an expressive individualism allied with Yankee utilitarianism, Bellah and his colleagues argue that "what has dropped out are the old normative expectations of what makes life worth living."[10] Here is where the evangelistic "itch" is in a very large chunk of American society. It is at the point where affluence and the failure to achieve self-fulfillment through fixation on the self intersect. It is at the point where Jesus argued that a person could not save the self and indulge the self at the same time. The rub here, however, is that one can scratch this itch only with the Cross.

It is too early to predict how the church will respond to this. If current styles and programs prevail, however, we will continue to grow churches with the same therapeutic orientation. We will continue to produce churches populated with believers who spiritualize and privatize their passions and who leave the social order to the politicians. One thing is clear: faith in Jesus Christ the Lord allows for no escapist "religious transcendence." Christian discipleship is not avertive in its outworking. It is thoroughly transformational and reformational.[11]

The challenge this poses for pastoral leadership, and that should include lay leaders as well, is to seek the conversion of the churches to the reformational character of their disciplines. Most denominations have a history of evangelism that has been wedded to the larger agenda of social change. This was especially true before these groups became mainline and established, when they were, in fact, the poor and marginal in society. If it can be demonstrated that one reason for their loss of a transformational emphasis, indeed their nominality, is affluence, it may be the time to convert them to the Scripture that says,

> Command those who are rich in this present world not to be arrogant nor to put their hope in wealth, which is so uncertain, but to put their hope in God, who richly provides us with everything for our enjoyment. Command them to do good, to be rich in good deeds, and to be generous and willing to share. In this way they will lay up treasure for themselves as a firm foundation for the coming age, so that they may take hold of the life that is truly life (1 Tim 6:17–19).

NOTES

[1]Rutilio Grande *El Salvador*, 36.

[2]Timothy Smith, *Theories of Nationalism*, (New York: Harper and Row, 1971), 3.

[3]Sami Hadawi, *Bitter Harvest: Palestine 1914–1979* (Delmar, N. Y.: Caravan Books, 1979), 196.

[4]Lesslie Newbigin, "Mission in the '80s," *International Bulletin of Missionary Research* (October 1980): 154.

[5]J. P. V. D. Balsdon, *Romans and Aliens* (Chapel Hill: Univ. of North Carolina Press, 1979), 12–14.

[6]Ibid., 2.

[7]"*Res publica* in general for those bonds of association and mutual commitment which exist between people who are joined together by ties of family or intimate associations; it is the bond of the crowd, of a 'people,' of a polity, rather than the bonds of family or of friends." Richard Sennett, *The Fall of Public Man* (New York: Knopf, 1977), 3.

[8]Ibid., 4.

[9]Quoted in Robert Bellah, *Habits of the Heart: Individualism and Commitment in American Life* (Berkeley: Univ. of California Press, 1987), 37.

[10]Ibid., 48.

[11]For a helpful view of these two options, see Nicholas Wolterstorff's *Until Justice and Peace Embrace* (Grand Rapids: Eerdmans, 1983).

4

Discipleship From the Bottom Up

On the surface Marks, Mississippi, looks like any other town in the Delta. To say "sleepy" would be to indulge in clichés and "laid back" is too Californian. Whatever else Marks may be, it is not California. But the town has its own rhythm as if an ancient hand had pressed the button marked "slo mo" and the pace of the society had changed gears.

The town is an old one and age, unlike people, does not discriminate. An outsider might get the impression that history, like an army in pursuit, had passed through the place leaving it stunned and stunted. Cotton, once the backbone of the economy, is no longer king, and the soil seems unable to bear all the burden of community life. The houses are neat for the most part, yet not the neatness that accompanies prosperity. It is, rather, that gritty neatness accomplished by marginal people whose daily life is a struggle against the erosion of history. The paint on their houses is tired, and even nature seems to have taken her moisture elsewhere, making the traditional Good Friday garden-planting even more an exercise in wishful thinking than faith.

In Marks you have to look hard to find the black community. Class distinctions are often blurred when marginality is the one thing people have in common. Black people, while comprising well over half the state's population, are not expected to be seen. They are invisible even though their shack-homes dot the countryside, much like the shacks in northern farm communities where migrant Mexicans labor over tomatoes and sugar beets.

To be sure, not all black people live in row houses here. But given the economic conditions, a more substantial dwelling is an exception. The median income for blacks in Quitman County in 1980 was $1,921, compared to $6,454 for white residents. There are no black bankers here, no black doctors or lawyers, no black merchant class. Young men and women whose talents could be translated into that kind of activity have long since left these parts. Their brothers and sisters will follow. At least those few who managed to eke out some semblance of education in these parts. In the Delta black education rarely survives beyond junior high, and those with enough talent and education to leave rarely return—except for family affairs and funerals.[1]

But the white community is suffering depression here also, and if white people are marginalized, then black people are nowhere. This is a fact the white community is careful to reinforce. In this county the clock is stuck somewhere between post-Reconstruction and that other civil war called the civil rights movement. White is still right in the estimation of those who wield power. It is no longer fashionable nor legally permissible to intimidate black people in the same manner as before. The movement changed all that. Fanny Lou Hamer changed all that. Ed Cole, the only black state chairman of a major political party in America, is changing all that.

But much of the change around here, in practical terms, is more style than substance. It is still possible to intimidate black people. After all, white people own that land on which those shacks rest. Substance still translates into psychological and economic domination of black people. In a state that ranks forty-ninth in per capita income and near the bottom of all the states in educational levels, it nevertheless ranks nearly twenty-fifth in millionaires per capita.

I had come to Marks to see the Reverend Carl Brown, a Baptist pastor and leader in the community. I had heard of him through the efforts of the Voice of Calvary ministries in Jackson and Mendenhall, which had assisted him in some community organization work. Pastor Brown had invited me to lunch, and before that took place I witnessed a historic handshake between Brown and a black lawyer who had come to finalize the papers granting the development association the right to build a new community center. This proposed center had been the center of a political storm in Marks. White leaders vehemently opposed it for fear it would upset the economic order that had prevailed there for generations. The black community, in a show of solidarity not seen since the heyday of the civil rights movement, boycotted the entire city of Marks for one month until the white power structure relented. Today that building houses a Thriftco Clothing Store, a laundromat, and new offices for the Development Organization and Credit Union.

We ate in a small restaurant that was part of the community project. The plate was piled high and the waitress smiled as she placed it in front of me. It was the same smile that accompanies a work of art. The fried chicken, the greens and black-eyed peas, the dressing—it all would be good and she knew it. She was right.

As we ate, I watched a badly misshapen man struggle across the highway. He was supported by a cane as he finally negotiated the steps of an old building that housed the grocery store, barber shop, and drug store. As we finished eating, the tall frame emerged from the old building and Pastor Brown, ever alert, asked whether I had observed him. My affirmation was followed by his remark, "That man's been hit several times by cars since his youth, else he'd be near seven feet tall. He's an interesting man. Most days he'll walk downtown, sit next to the sidewalk, and proceed to call white folks every kind of name he can think of. Then he'll get up and walk on back home."

"Why's he still alive," I asked.

"Most white people think he's crazy," he offered.

"Is he?" I asked, an answer already forming in my mind.

"Not so crazy as the white people think," he said, a mere hint of a smile on his broad face.

We ate in reflective silence broken occasionally by one of Brown's aides. A black pastor is usually busy, if he's the only pastor in town charged with the task of changing things. I didn't want to spend more of his time. My mind returned to the misshapen man. He was really still alive because, crazy or not, he posed no threat to the white power structure. No one needed to take him seriously. He had no power. Mr. Brown is another matter. So is Robert L. Jackson, coordinator of the Quitman County Development Organization. Not many years ago these men would have been run out of town. Or lynched.

Carl Brown can be viewed as dangerous. He was born in this town and grew up in the Baptist Church. After a twenty-five-year absence he has returned to pastor the church of his youth. Brown makes no threats, uses no profanity aimed at the white community. But in the past decade he has managed to challenge white bigotry and black apathy and mount a movement of self-determination among blacks in the county. In short, Brown and his colleagues have begun a power movement. The movement reached one of its high points when Jackson ran for the city council in 1983. He lost. But the campaign, which drew national recognition and brought Jesse Jackson to Marks, sent shock waves throughout the county, especially among whites. It reached its apogee in 1987 when Robert Jackson became the first black supervisor of District Two in Quitman County.

The pattern is a familiar one. A man of God responds to the spiritual needs of a people only to discover that life, their lives in the totality of the meaning of life, cannot be spiritualized. He realizes that the political and economic needs of people interface with their religious values. The people one seeks to serve may not know this, but the leadership comes to see it. Life lived on the margins of society requires leadership that understands a people's essential needs. The question a busy pastor must ask then is not how to make a struggling church grow, but how to empower a marginal people beaten down and wracked by self-doubt and not a little self-hatred. For as Kyle Haselden reminded us, white racism has denied the black person the right to be, not simply the right to belong or to have.[2] It is this denial of the right to be that locates the essential challenge of the gospel and its attendant ministries.

The resolution of the challenge, to empower the powerless, begins with presence. In a fine doctoral work on the early ministry of various urban missionaries, Norris Magnuson reveals that "what ultimately gave gospel welfare organizations their strongest insight and motivation for service was the continuing close contact of their field workers with the poor." Using a quote from an early edition of the *British War Cry*, Magnuson comments of Emma Bown, who in 1895 headed up the Salvation Army's slum work in America, "She probably knows more of American slum life than any other woman in the world."[3]

Jesus commanded his followers to go into all the world, to all the nations. This is not a command to throw tracts at people (as we once did in the dark ages of a zealous fundamentalism) nor even to pitch a tent and have a revival meeting. (Nowadays this "tent" is really an auditorium complete with air conditioning and kleig lights for the television cameras and film crews. The old camp meeting has gone uptown.) This isn't exactly what Jesus had in mind. Since going is followed by teaching, it is clear that a sustained relationship with a people is envisioned. Even what we call preaching, if it is isolated from presence, is not the model here. Presence is what he had in mind in giving the command.

It is commonplace in many poor communities in Mississippi to have churches without resident pastors. They are served on a monthly or bimonthly basis by pastors who commute from cities often as far away as a hundred miles. Often these men hold regular jobs during the week and preach on Sundays. The pattern is an economic necessity, for the most part, but not entirely. It is also the result of a failure to realize that the issue of ministry is not merely preaching, marrying, and burying. Ministry is also the empowerment of one's people. I would argue that this is done through spiritual direction, and that requires a presence, a solidarity, with people in all their struggles.

I don't mean to minimize the economic factors that dictate certain limitations on ministry. Rather, I want to argue that pastoral presence must address the economic issue as part of empowerment, and this cannot be done by commuting. For many black preachers this is a catch-22 situation. The way around it is modeled by Jesus and his coworkers. They lived off the land, shared a common purse, accepted the hospitality of people of good will. In short, they moved in for the long haul. This too, must be seen as part and parcel of what it means to be spiritual.

Of course, Jesus did preach. His was a threefold ministry. He preached, he taught, and he healed. In one astounding instruction, he told some followers of John the Baptist that one sure sign of his authenticity as the Christ was that "the poor have good news preached to them" (Luke 7:22, RSV). Strange statement. Disappointing? On the surface surely, for the last thing poor people need is to be preached to. Especially if the preacher is bent on accusing them one more time of moral failure as a cause of their plight in society.

But Jesus knew something about preaching that has been forgotten in our time, at least among many Anglo church leaders: preaching is an event, to be sure, God commanding light to shine out of darkness. But it is more. Preaching is solidarity with a people, a declaration that God and the preacher are one with the hearers. Paul made this point on several occasions; "we were willing to give you not the gospel only, but also our very lives" (1 Thess. 2:8). He says this again in 2 Corinthians 4:2 where he claims that the preacher and the truth are inseparable. The association of preaching with the poor had to be perceived by Christ's hearers as consonant with the gospel he preached and the new order he announced. The poor, the blind, the lame, the deaf—in short, those who had no power—were the recipients of the gift of the good news, and with that proclamation another indication of the eternal bias of God toward the nobodies of the earth.

Preaching also signals to society that a new order has come. It is eschatological in nature. It is powerful in its effect. The gospel is not mere words. When Jesus replied to the Pharisees' criticism after he had healed the paralytic, he seemed to be saying in effect, "If we are merely dealing with words, then it is just as easy to say 'Get up and walk' as to say, 'Your sins are forgiven.'" Then, to demonstrate that he was not playing mere word games, he spoke the words that freed the man from his bondage. His word was power and demonstration that a new order had come into their midst.

In the book of Leviticus, good news of the Jubilee Year was heralded by trumpets. Prison doors were thrown open, debts were forgiven, and new beginnings were celebrated. Jesus' preaching was not accompanied with any of this fanfare and he rode no powerful stallion into town. But the poor people heard him gladly. They knew he was one of them. They could tell it because, though he was clearly on a mission to Jerusalem, he was not just passing by on a stroll. He knew them. His stories were their stories, their enemies his. He walked among them through their fields, fished with them in their waters, ate in their homes, shopped their markets. He blew no trumpet, but he was present. Preaching may not be the whole task of the minister, but it is one way that leadership demonstrates its solidarity with the oppressed. For to preach well, with integrity, one must be truly present.

Presence is a many-sided reality. There is, of course, the presence of a leader in a situation of ministry. The sent one has come: Paul, Priscilla, and Aquila in Corinth; Titus in Troas; Timothy in Macedonia. Earlier it was Peter in Caesarea at the house of Cornelius. There can be no work of God apart from the incarnational presence of the minister of God. Not even the voice of an angel in the prayer chamber of Cornelius is adequate. Peter must be sent for. Paul drives this home by his near-rhetorical question to the Roman believers, ". . . and how shall they hear without a preacher?" (Rom. 10:14)

Another dimension of Christian presence among the earth's peoples is that of the sending community. As Paul put it, "How shall they preach except they be sent?" Yet it is imperative that we recognize that the prior sending committee is the Triune God. Jesus delighted in referring to himself as the sent one, claiming that even the words he spoke were not his own, but those of "him who sent me" (John 6:38, 57; 7:16–18). His commission to his disciples in John 20 is hauntingly powerful: "As the Father has sent me, even so I send you."

Thus the task of the evangelist does not begin with him or her. It begins with and is defined by the holy community of God. The good news is God's and so also is the enterprise of the kingdom. Thus we enter into God's ministry in the world. This is why Jesus could claim that his efforts in behalf of the woman of Samaria were the work of the Father, for "the Father seeks such to worship him." The work of the missionary is significant only because God is the sending committee.

Then, too, Christian presence must mean a believing community. Evangelism and discipleship must have as its goal the establishing or the strengthening of a Christian society. Without the presence of a believing community there is no point to discipleship and no hope of any radical transformation in society. The gospel is not good news unless it can be seen to create a new humanity in the earth. Not simply new persons, one by one as the old hymns used to argue. But a new people, a new collective. And that new humanity is part and parcel of the good news. In the presence of God's people it is possible to see the grace of God (Acts 11:23).

For a people to be empowered means that they must discern the sources of those pressures that shape their daily lives. Empowerment assumes some pedagogical process. Borrowing from the work of the late C. Wright Mills, I contend that the citizen needs "lucid understanding" of the world around him or her. If the citizen needs this, so also does the believer, especially among the poor. Mills argued that in "an age of fact information often dominates their attention and dominates their capacity to assimilate it." What was needed, Mills contended, was what he called "the sociological imagination . . . a quality of mind that will help them to use information and to develop reason in order to achieve lucid summations of what is going on in the world and of what may be happening in themselves."[4] Mills felt certain that people know that they need this ability but are not well served by their leaders in attaining it. What he identified is called "conscientization" in another context and in another time.

What is going on in the world is trouble. I like Mills's understanding of the relationship between troubles and issues.

Trouble, according to Mills, is personal. An issue is more corporate and social. When a particular man is out of work, he and his family are probably in trouble. When fifteen percent of the work force and nearly seventy-five percent of young people are unemployed, that is an issue. If a teenager is pregnant, that can be trouble to an entire family. But if sixty percent of all babies born in the county are born out of wedlock, that is an issue. Leadership needs to help people make the connections between troubles and issues. Leadership must make the connections between issues and the larger historical scene in which the personal lives of people are being lived out. It is the responsibility of leaders to know and show how that history affects the ability of others in that society to make choices on their own behalf.

There can be no doubt that many people in urban life are in trouble by their own designs. Many are in prison because they would not "do right." But what can that mean if, according to the Source Book of Criminal Justice Statistics (June 30, 1984), forty percent of those jailed in local and county jails nationwide are black and another thirteen percent are Hispanic, or that ninety percent of those incarcerated in prisons have a history of childhood abuse? But the nonprison population, by far the majority, are often hurting because they do not know what is happening around them in the larger society and the world at large and how these events bear upon their daily existence.

The plant closing with no advance notice may be in the best interest of the company, but it certainly leaves people in deep trouble. But that decision was made because of global market pressures. It had nothing to do with the performances of the work force locally. In other words, "Don't take this personally. We simply can't compete with Taiwan." But when these scattered instances become a pattern and thousands of people are affected, especially white middle-class people, then troubles become issues and the issue is taken up by Congress.

When Uzi machine guns and other lethal weapons hitherto available only to armed forces in the military are bought over the counter by gang members or their supporters in south-central Los Angeles, the community needs some answers from its leaders. Why are Israel and Hong Kong, the sources of these armaments, not held accountable? How can the Jewish community of Los Angeles accuse a black American running for the presidency in 1988 of anti-Semitism and be silent about this gunrunning from Israel, the same guns that find their way to white armies in South Africa? In such circumstances the pastoral task must include some sensitizing of one's membership to what is going on. Leaders of the church should be in touch with law enforcement, lawmakers, labor, management, and political and civic leaders in order to be able to offer help and to serve as a possible agent for reconciliation. It is this activity that Vincent Cosmao identifies with the gospel:

> The Gospel message passes judgment on the world, not to condemn it, but to save it. It brings to light what is hidden, and what can continue to function only insofar as it remains invisible. The Gospel summons us to analyze reality, even as Jesus did. When Jesus commented on the tie between Caesar and his coinage, he made clear the vanity of Caesar's pretensions to divinity: A tax collector no longer had any right to make demands in the name of divine worship.[5]

Can we find a model for such activity in Jesus? Indeed. Consider his teaching about the rich. "Woe to you that are rich, for you have received your consolation. . . . Woe to you who are full now, for you shall hunger" (Luke 6:24–25, RSV). Or his celebrated story of the rich man and the poor beggar. Or his encounter with the notorious tax-gatherer, Zacchaeus. Of course not all rich people in the narratives were villains. Only most of them. Jesus does not seem to level a blanket condemnation of riches per se, nor of those who possess them. But his stories uniformly warn against trusting in wealth and could not help but alert his hearers to his knowledge that private wealth usually translates into public control.

Cosmao is helpful here also. His Thesis 11 states that "Left to their own inertia, societies come to be structured in terms of inequality"[6]. He develops his argument by observing that this is partly due to the "asymmetry of human relationships" and observes that this asymmetry is often the stuff of enthnological investigation. "Ethnologists talk glibly about 'jealousy' or 'envy' when they refer to this keen sense of equality [among traditional groups with a degree of stability]; superficial observers see only the tendency toward leveling and mediocrity. A more profound analysis suggests that the relative equality of such societies is the result of voluntary strategies for regulating social relationships."[7]

These regulators of social relationships are those who, by virtue of birth and privilege, inherit the prevailing or predominant traditional apparatus. It's another way of saying that they who make the definitions control the agenda. Heaven help the poor soul not bright enough to be born so as to take advantage of the access to opportunity.

It follows from this that in order to maintain this position of privilege, people with power deem it necessary to seek sanction from the gods. Hence the intensity of the criticism Jesus leveled at certain religious leaders of his day. He was especially hard on the Pharisees, the traditionalists, who, more than others, were seen as the keepers of the cultural flame. This was their image of themselves also.

Jesus knew that these leaders were often in league with the wealthy and the politicians and, in some instances, provided religious sanctions for their oppressive policies. He also knew that the people knew who these leaders were and how they operated. It was crucial that they know that he knew if he was to break them out of their captivity to the system. For the system, to borrow from Paul Tillich, is wedded to the past, especially when it is attached to the "myth of origin"[8] as in Judaism. Jesus knew that systems, especially in periods of social unrest, need priests to validate their claims of allegiance among the masses. These priests need to be trained and thus schools are created, benefits added, special garments designed to set them farther apart from the masses. They get favored status from the wealthy and those whom the wealthy support in office.

Jesus knew of the tendency among the more conservative among them to argue that their conservatism derived from Scripture when in fact it developed from an adherence to man-made tradition. Thus Jesus blasted them more than once for destroying the credibility of the Word of God in the eyes of the people through their rigid allegiance to tradition and their lust for power. He scored them for their unbelief, claiming that faith was impossible so long as their overriding concern was for "the favor of men rather than the favor of God" (John 5:44). One of the reasons the common people heard him gladly was because he said outloud what they all knew by observation and by well-honed instincts. They talked about these things in their homes, even though they were not topics of conversation in the synagogues. Thus there began to emerge from his teachings a profound pedagogy aimed at the peasants, those to whom he said, "the kingdom belongs to you" (Luke 6:20).

But Jesus was not naïve about the poor. He knew of their propensities to greed. They too were human and when they were faced with having things and using power, they did not distinguish themselves from those who were more favored and had better access to privilege. Thus Jesus warned against covetousness even among the poor. But the point is that Jesus questioned the so-called benefactors of the people and revealed how phony were their claims to be serving the people. He carefully showed how even the Roman presence was not the critical factor that determined the quality of their lives. That critical factor had to be within them. They needed inner moral strength and with it they could even carry the armor of the enemy an extra mile. They could learn to pray for the enemy or turn the other cheek when struck. In so doing they would avoid what, for the disciple, is the most undesirable outcome— becoming like the enemy. Disciples are called to be like their heavenly Father.

But if Jesus was hard on the conservatives of his day, he was also unyielding in his denunciation of those who would seek a violent solution to the woes of the people. All sorts of efforts have been put forth in recent years to make of Jesus some sort of religious guerrilla, dedicated to a religious-political solution to the Jewish dilemma. The arguments of such revolutionaries are often attractive. If one is part of an oppressed community, the ideas set forth in their appeals are often enticing. Who wouldn't be excited about discovering some sanction for getting rid of the oppressor by any means necessary, especially if that sanction comes from someone who speaks for God?

What made this option so attractive in Israel was the great prophetic tradition that had sustained the people for centuries. Jewish history from the beginning was a litany that could have been sung with the words of the '60s anthem, "We Shall Overcome." God was with these people and would fight for them. As Michael Lerner puts it, "The notion that the world could and should be different than it is has deep roots within Judaism. It is this refusal to take the world as given, articulated in the Prophetic call for transformation, that has fueled the radical underpinnings of Jewish life."[9] But it is often a small step from this contention to the great tradition of the Maccabees, or the lesser revered history of men who mistook their political ambitions for the divine will. Violence, even in the prophetic tradition, is problematic.

Jesus is clearly within the Jewish prophetic tradition. He would smile with recognition and pleasure at Lerner's words, "To the Prophets, God's message directed attention to daily life, to the marketplace, to the family and to the state. To the Prophets, each time the powerless were oppressed was a fresh outrage, each time religion was used as a cover for economic immorality was a new affront to God."[10] It may well be that the current failure of much of the church to grasp the prophetic significance of Jesus is due to its blindness to his Jewishness and to the teaching of Paul that the church is built on the prophets. Thus we miss the this-worldly aspect of the kingdom order. Lerner has this to say:

> The commitment to change the world, to demand justice in a world that has given up on these ideals, is not some pious sentiment clouding one's eyes to a hard-nosed look at reality. On the contrary, the rejection of moral neutrality, the committed stance on behalf of the oppressed, makes possible a deeper understanding of the dynamics of culture and society. It is precisely in the process of acting to transform the world that the world reveals its deeper structures and meanings.[11]

105

Yet Jesus clearly did not allow his followers to choose violence in the service of the kingdom. Speaking directly to the question of his kingship, and by implication, his willingness to use force if necessary to establish his reign, Jesus replied, "My kingdom is not of this world. If it were, my servants would fight to prevent my arrest by the Jews. But now my kingdom is from another place" (John 18:36).

Jesus is not employing a rhetorical strategy in making this claim. He is not simply buying time, stringing the debate out until his forces gather courage and storm the palace gate. Neither is he confessing to a defenseless position as one forsaken by his God and his followers. He is clearly not defenseless; rather he is undefending. In this way Jesus bears testimony that his kingdom is not run according to the values of this world. He is certainly not saying, as many modern evangelicals have him saying, that his reign has nothing to do with the pain of this world. The very presence in this world of the King argues powerfully that God does care about the world and that the new order is intended to be right smack in the middle of it all.

But the kingdom, even though it is in the middle of it all, does not set its course by the world's values. It does not subscribe to its reasons or patterns for behavior. If this were not so, Jesus argued, "my disciples would fight."

This world is run by greed for power and for status. Its people seek primarily to find the good life. But Christ's new order, in its pastoral, priestly, and prophetic expressions is not of this world; it doesn't operate on these motivations and values, does not borrow from this historic tendency in the human race. The character of the kingdom is both spiritual and social but profoundly and primarily ethical. For this reason it cannot be reduced to simple formulas under the rubric of evangelism. By its very nature, the kingdom is a rejection of moral neutrality.

The rejection of moral neutrality may be said to be the beginning of discipleship. The key word is "repent," and it is clear from a reading of Scripture that this is more than a private matter. It *is* intensely personal; it *is not* private. John the Baptist, for instance, made it clear that to be in right relationship with God was to get things straight with one's contemporaries (Luke 3:3–14).[12] The demand was specific: restitution must be equal to the offense and according to the need of one's fellow. The social demand is unavoidable.

Repentance is certainly the beginning of conversion and the doorway to transformation. Following the argument set forth by Beasley-Murray, repentance and faith are the "unexpected corollary" to Christ's revelation of the kingdom as being "within the reach" of everyone; it "lies within their power to enter it and secure its blessings"[13]. For this reason it is also the beginning of a new humanity in the earth among those who make the choice; a new community that, if it conforms to the provisions of the kingdom of grace, will demonstrate in its relationships with one another the many-faceted wisdom of God (Eph. 3:10).

NOTES

[1]According to a bulletin from the Quitman County Development Organization, Inc., "the median school years completed for persons over twenty-five years of age is only eight years. The corresponding figures for Black males was 4.4 and for Black females only 6.2."

[2]Kyle Haselden, *The Racial Problem in Christian Perspective* (New York: Harper and Row, 1959).

[3]Norris Magnuson, *Salvation in the Slums: Evangelical Social Welfare Work 1865–1920*, ATLA Monograph Series no. 10 (Metuchen, N. J.: Scarecrow, 1977), 32.

[4]C. Wright Mills, "The Promise of the Sociological Imagination" in *The Relevance of Sociology*, ed. Jack D. Douglas (New York: Appleton-Century-Crofts, 1970), 5–10.

[5]Vincent Cosmao, *Changing the World*, trans. John Drury (Maryknoll, N. Y.: Orbis, 1977), 58.

[6]Ibid., 34.

[7]Ibid., 35.

[8]Paul Tillich, *The Socialist Decision*, trans. Franklin Sherman (New York: Harper and Row, 1977), 1–26.

[9]Michael Lerner, "Tikkun," *A Quarterly Jewish Critique of Politics, Culture, and Society*, no. 1 (1980): 3.

[10]Ibid., 4.

[11]Ibid., 3–4.

[12]G. R. Beasley-Murray, *Jesus and the Kingdom of God* (Grand Rapids: Eerdmans, 1986), 102–3.

[13]Ibid.

5

Gettin' It On—Together

If transformation begins with repentance, it is borne along by faith and hope. The preaching of John and Jesus, and before them the announcements from the angels to their respective parents, did more than provoke repentance and confession of sins. It also triggered a new hope (Titus 1:1–2). Oppressed peoples from Palestine to Mississippi need hope. At least they need the faint hope that is in them, especially if it has religious roots, to be validated. It is a curious thing to have this hope rekindled by the fiery preaching of a holy man who demands of the oppressed that they get their ethical lives together and that the well-off (those with two shirts and more food than they can eat) share their bounty with the have-nots (Luke 3:7–14). In short, hope is born, or reborn, when spiritual transformation begins. It is a sign that God is active among his people, and if God be for us—well, anything is possible, even in Nazareth. Or Marks, Mississippi.

To hear God's judgment upon one's sins conveys to the oppressed that God takes them seriously. In a society where it is difficult to be taken seriously by anyone, and where there are very few reasons to be responsible for one's actions, it may be as refreshing as a cold splash of water in the face to hear that the God of all creation not only notices you, but also takes you and your conduct seriously—even personally. As the civil rights movement gained both momentum and insight, it began to announce the good news to black Americans: "You are somebody."[1] It is a profound theological idea.

Everybody is somebody. This is an idea that runs right through the biblical record. It is grounded in the creation of human beings in the image of God; it is sustained in the cross of God's Son. Of course the idea is bastardized (like most good ideas). To be sure, it has led to cultural chauvanisms and the cult of narcissism, even to nationalistic idolatry. But each human being *is* somebody, and the oppressed, more than others, need to know that God knows they are. If this is not so, then the poor may be tempted to think that God is the author of their negative self-images, that God was biased toward the privileged. Perhaps even toward a white racist.

Transformation in one's life and in the life of an entire society requires a change in one's self-understanding. It is important, in calling people to obedience inspired by faith, to announce the good news that God is excited about the prospect of being in right relationship with them. If Uncle Sam doesn't want you, God does. The cross testifies to that. The demand to change and turn around must be heard at the depths of one's being. It must be heard also as a reassurance that God's eye is on the sparrow and that he is prepared to take up the cause of those who align themselves with his enterprise.

But taking sides with God, especially against oneself, is costly. And the cost is part and parcel of the initial proclamation. Indeed, it is often the perceived cost of following Jesus that dissuades people from making a commitment to him. Thus, the gospel is at once both enticing and repellant. To the human spirit it is both good news and bad news; good news in that it promises forgiveness and eternal life, bad news in that it demands an unconditional surrender to the author of that good news; good news in that it promises that God is with us, bad news in that God will hold us accountable for the way we behave in the light of new marching orders. Faithfulness to God and the gospel, let alone the person to whom we minister, allows us no freedom to mask this demand.

The Lausanne Covenant catches this truth in its paragraph, "The nature of evangelism." After defining evangelism as proclamation with a view to persuading persons to come to Jesus Christ, the document argues that "in issuing the invitation we have no liberty to conceal the cost of discipleship." David Bosch, in arguing against the tendency among people whose chief value is the numerical growth of the church, states that "Authentic evangelism may in fact cause people not to join the church, because of the cost involved."[2] Any call to faith in Jesus Christ is at the same time a call to obedience to him as Lord of life.

Obedience to Jesus Christ is not an option. Jesus always made it clear that he demanded all of life and that any attempt to "save" one's life at his expense was to lose it (Luke 9:23–27). The apostle Paul understood this principle as an integral part of his calling. To the Romans he exulted, "We received grace and apostleship to call people from among all the Gentiles to the obedience that comes from faith" (1:5). This is the point of the commission that Jesus gave his people. They were to go into all the world and "make disciples of all nations." They were to baptize and to teach as part of the discipling process. The emphasis here is not on evangelism as it is popularly used in the West. We tend to use the term as indicating the church's entire task, and when wedded to bumper-sticker-like slogans such as "evangelize the world in this generation" the impression is sustained that evangelism is the end product as well as the means.

This distorted view of evangelism cannot be sustained by the Scriptures. The favorite text in support of evangelism, Matthew 28:18–20, is clearly an admonition to make disciples. The key verb in that passage is *matheteusate*, which means "make disciples." The other verbs or verb forms in the passage, translated "go," "baptize," "teach" serve only to support and elaborate upon this central imperative. The objective is always making disciples. What is popularly called evangelism is simply the means to that end.

Exegetically, it is important to see that the popular passage from Matthew commanding the making of disciples is understood by Jesus as part of his kingdom emphasis. Indeed contemporary scholars see this passage as the focus from which the entire Gospel of Matthew must be seen.[3] Discipleship then, is the process by which converts are shaped by the values and power of the new reign of God. To interpret this commission outside this context is to miss his intention in evangelizing. To make disciples in the light of the new reign of God is to demand of one's hearers that they obey his kingdom teaching and practice justice in all their social dealings. This is the meaning of the "all things I have commanded you" in the passage.

Whether speaking to an adulterous woman or blasting her accusers for their failure to understand mercy, Jesus made it clear that to take him seriously was to change. A concern for the poor was related to the "things you ought to have done," evidently part of the tradition that was being ignored by the religious leaders (Luke 11:39–42). Further, his call to discipleship was always a clear demand that the convert forsake all to follow him. What that means is often spelled out (see Luke 9:57–62 and Mark 10:17–22).

Jesus sought with his disciples, before anything else, to establish his authority. There will be a new community, new relationships, a new agenda for the people of God. But first there must be the recognition of and submission to a new leader. One chief and many members of a new tribe. This is the one way to ensure against discipleship becoming another fad, another attempt of entrepreneurs to huckster the mission for profit, another product for cassette distribution. Discipleship is the objective of all our evangelistic efforts. If the church needs to rediscover this in our time, so be it. But it is nothing new. Jesus clearly taught this and in his last appearances commanded his people to disciple the nations. But he also demonstrated in all his ministry that this was by far the most radical and efficient way to transform humankind. Discipleship and transformation are closely related, as close as cause and effect.

To say this is to court the displeasure of those who have long dissociated discipleship from matters dealing with social transformation. To them discipleship is purely a spiritual matter, the goal of which is Christlikeness in one's personal life and intimate relationships. This version is certainly a part of the package. It is clear from the teachings and practice of Jesus that radical change had to do with persons, and the basic unit was the individual. To hear his conversations with individuals ranging from Zacchaeus and Nicodemus to the woman of Samaria is to be aware of his understanding of the radical nature of personal conversion. But it is also clear that he understood how these personal biographies related to the larger social milieu (the broader networks of relationships, customs, institutions, etc.) and how that milieu in turn shaped the individuals within that context.

After all, the woman in John 4 was a woman of Samaria! A woman. Of Samaria. Simply to say that is to realize that whatever salvation means to her, it is far more than merely a private matter. And what follows in that narrative indicates the profound social nature of her personal transformation.

The single mother on welfare living in the overcrowded confines of a roach-infested downtown tenement building in Los Angeles may need to be saved, but her social milieu needs transformation as well. What is needed in her milieu is different from what is needed in the milieu of a female single parent in Bel Air. The differences can be illustrated by considering the explosion of evangelical interest in the family—marriage, child rearing, etc. While a focus on these issues is extremely important, the movement to make the family over is basically a middle- and upper-middle class concern. They are the ones who have time to listen to radio, subscribe to magazines, and relate to counselors in air-conditioned offices. It is not that the lower classes do not care about their families or the prospect of a solid marriage. It is simply that the factors affecting this possibility are much different for them than for their more comfortable neighbors across town. Any attempt to transform their milieu must take account of that.

The factors that always must be taken into account are educational, economic, and most certainly political. An urban rabbi working the asphalt today might wonder what a focus on the family would look like there. If the church cannot demonstrate that the gospel, and hence discipleship, can address their total situation, then the church forfeits its greatest opportunity

113

and in the process misrepresents the gospel. To transform a social milieu means to begin with a realistic understanding of how people are actually having to live before trying to help them move toward a new goal. And, of course, it should be clear that the good news must take the form of the new community of grace and love.

But tying discipleship to transformation brings more than the disfavor of those who see the church's task in "spiritual" terms. It brings the risk of venturing into solidarity with people who are not "our kind." In this venture there is the possibility that in such a relationship the evangelist may get converted. This comes about when she realizes that the socially disadvantaged are often made so by factors outside their control, by people outside their control. What control do poor people have over the "fourteen families" of El Salvador or their counterparts in any major urban center throughout the world? To identify with the victims of greed could get one in serious trouble.

The history of urban mission reveals this pattern. Solidarity always led to some form of conscientization for the evangelist. This usually came about from interaction with the urban poor and a clash between the evangelist's objective situation and formal training on the one hand and the reality of the new situation on the other. Thus a Walter Rauschenbusch could confess that nothing he had learned in seminary had prepared him for Hells Kitchen. Thus a Catherine Booth, while deeply committed to personal holiness, argued passionately for social reform. She knew, by experience, that social ills could not be addressed by mere charity. The need was for justice.[4]

The fact is—and here is the real risk—that solidarity with marginal peoples tends to convert the evangelist to a larger agenda, something one's theology does not naturally do. Nothing in all his progress through seminary life on the way to the priesthood prepared Rutilio Grande for his education among the poor in his own country. The reasons for this are many, but the chief one is that the issue for people in power, including those who operate seminaries, is the maintenance of their own power. Thus theological questions about the realities tend not to be encouraged. This is because such questions are raised in institutions supported by those of wealth and power and that, by their very nature, might challenge that position of wealth and power.

The late Archbishop Romero and his friend Rutilio Grande would put it another way. They would say that religion is the key to dealing with injustice, but not the religion of the bourgeoisie; not the religion of "the families," those who rule and call the shots. To say this is to risk getting killed, but that is essentially why Jesus was killed. A religion that takes as its starting point the plight of the poor, especially when poverty is the result of injustice, has always put its practitioners in jeopardy. As long as religion was in the hands of the priests, Pharisees, and that glut of establishment types, nothing was going to happen in Israel. When it became clear that the young rabbi was attracting the masses to his radical teachings, the plot was hatched to do him in.

What then would a transformation movement look like? I am attracted to the way Vincent Harding puts this question:

> Beginning with ourselves, beginning where we are, what must we tear down, what must we build up, what foundations must we lay? Who shall we work with, what visions can we create, what hopes shall possess us? How shall we organize? How shall we be related to those in South Africa, in El Salvador, in Guyana? How shall we communicate with others the urgency of our time? How shall we envision and work for the revolutionary transformation of our own country? What are the inventions, the discoveries, the new concepts that will help us move toward the revolution we need in this land?[5]

Harding is writing out of the pain occasioned by the murder of the fine Guyanese scholar Walter Rodney and the struggle among Afro-Caribbean and Afro-Americans to find a way past the restricting forms and definitions of Euro-American culture. The approach implicit in his questions may not be the precise starting point of the work of transformation, but it is close. The questions he poses are pertinent to people on the periphery as well as those at the center. So what would be some of the salient features of an evangelical movement of transformation?

One characteristic of such a movement would be a strong orientation to the Scriptures. Any ministry of transformation must be consolidated by a disciplined study of the Word of God. Spiritual direction in the service of the kingdom derives its focus from the Scriptures. Converts can follow their new leader only if they know and come to understand his ways. This is true not only for new converts but also for those in leadership positions. Moses knew this well and begged God, "Teach me your ways so that I may know you and continue to find favor with you" (Ex. 33:13). This knowledge of God and favor with him was in order that God's people would be served. "Remember that this nation is your people," Moses concluded.

From one end of Scripture to the other, leadership among God's people is defined in terms of servanthood and a crucial feature of that role was that the minister be able to commend the Word of God to the learning and obedience of the people of God. Failure in this task was taken as an indication that such leadership had forfeited its calling. Any refusal on the part of people to obey the teaching of the Word of God was taken as a rejection of God. This principle can be traced from Moses through the prophets to Jesus and the apostles.

And what if the new converts cannot read? J. Alfred Smith is pastor of one of the country's important congregations. It has become a pillar in Oakland, California, through his strength and courageous leadership. When he introduced me recently, I responded by sharing some insights about evangelism to the large class. When I had finished, one of Dr. Smith's parishioners rose to say that he had just performed an act of evangelism. "I just gave a Bible to a man during the meeting," he said. I recall having seen the man. He had come in off the street earlier on in the class session. He was probably not a member of Allen Temple.

The parishioner wanted me to comment on his act, and more importantly, on whether his act was evangelism. I fudged the answer. "Let me switch hats for a moment," I said. "I'll be a professor now. It is important to give the Word of God to

116

people. But let me ask this: could the man read what you gave him?" The would-be evangelist revealed from his expression that he had not thought of this. Of course simply handing out the Bible does not constitute evangelism.

In some segments of our society, especially in our urban centers, the ability to read is a major social issue. If people cannot read, can they really be drawn into the process of transformation? As another church member in another place said, "I have come to know that God has sent me a love letter, the Bible, and I couldn't read it. So I went to school to learn to read." The man was in his sixties, and, as a result of this new skill, his faith was being transformed.

If the people of God cannot read, they must be taught to read. The weight of biblical experience is that without the knowledge of God's Word people perish; they have no direction except that supplied by their own wits and their own culture. "Is there any word from God?" is more than the inquiry of an anxious and power-drunk politician (Jer. 37:17). It is the cry of the human spirit quickened by the Spirit of God, a cry more primal than that of a deer panting for water.

Another goal of a movement of transformation is the forming and encouraging of disciplined minds to interpret the Scriptures. The step from illiteracy (or, for that matter, ignorance of the Word) to an understanding of the Scriptures is the beginning of a practical theology. This is more than teaching people to memorize Scripture, as important as that is. It is, rather, an exercise in training converts to understand what the Scriptures mean for their particular situation.

In developing disciplined minds several key realizations will emerge. The first is that one's life situation plays an important part in determining what the Scriptures mean. People come to the text from different starting points. One's views of God may be strongly affected if one has been abused by one's own father. A Samaritan would hear the text differently from a Jew, and that same Samaritan would find it difficult to hear any text expounded by a Jew. The new convert will likely come to the text with suspicion of anything or anyone connected with his or her experience of being domi-

117

nated. She may not know this in a rational, conscious way. But this hermeneutic is at work at deep subconscious levels, and as deep calls to deep a new consciousness begins to awaken.

That novices in the faith are wary is understandable. As John De Cruchy puts it, history is rife with examples of the co-option of theology for the uses of political and ideological elites. These

> so-called "theologies from above" . . . reflect the ideology of those in power, those who rule from above, and thereby reinforce structures of domination. They are the theologies of the court theologians and prophets who serve the interests of the state and the cultus. They are theologies of uncritical patriotism, theologies which are not committed to hearing the living word of the Lord today in our present crisis and context.[6]

I have seen this suspicion of court theologians, evangelists, and missiologists in every urban center I have known for the past thirty years. As the reader has become aware, I share the suspicion. Victims of injustice, when exposed to Christians whose theories seem not to address their situation, begin to realize that a distance exists between their "experience" of the text, and the interpretation of similar texts by those of the dominant culture. It is for this reason that attempts on the part of church leaders to demote social ethics in the interests of church growth are suspect. Postponed ethics, an inevitable result of the "discipling" and "perfecting" scheme set forth by McGavran and Wagner, tend to remain postponed, especially given humanity's celebrated talent for selectively responding to ethical demands.

Furthermore, as Andrew Kirk has pointed out, this tendency to put asunder what God hath joined is another instance of faulty methodology. While acknowledging that statements such as the Lausanne Covenant cannot tell the whole story of the church's mission, Kirk argues that for that very reason such statements should reflect a "thorough interpretation of all the relevant material." For Kirk, and for many of us, this is what is missing in both evangelical and ecumenical circles. "Both groups appeal to a condensed view of Scriptural teaching.

Elements that do not fit into the traditional pattern are ignored or discarded. The result is a distortion on both sides of the task of evangelism.'"[7]

Churches grow in the black community on Chicago's South Side, and to the uninitiated they seem to grow along homogeneous lines. But growth is not the central issue there. Justice is. Poverty is. Drugs and substandard housing are, and violence of all sorts. Theories of growth and the devotional theology offered by area seminaries and Bible institutes do not help much in providing them with an adequate understanding of how to wage war against the powers of deceit and inhumanity in that city. For a people "in the times" rather than "above the times," the black church has had to develop a theology from within its setting, and it is a practical theology.

The idea of a new community reflecting on its situation from a scriptural position and being willing to put into practice what God gives them out of his Word is revolutionary. It works because it takes place among people who are trying to make sense out of what is often a senseless life situation. I suspect that it is for this reason that many of these Christians prefer the Old Testament as a starting point rather than the New, and certainly more than the epistles of Paul. The reason has nothing to do with esoteric theories of scholars who think they see in Paul something different from what they see in Jesus and the gospels. For most Christians who may be just beginning to think for themselves in the Scriptures, the key is simpler than that.

The Old Testament is full of stories that are the record of people struggling to find an identity and a meaning for their lives amidst the harsh vagaries of life. It is fundamentally a story of redemption and deliverance. Furthermore, these stories lend themselves to an oral tradition, a tradition often perpetuated to their detriment by a lack of access to education. Also, the people in these stories are simple folk, often poor, scarcely able to fend for themselves. Some are wealthy, struggling to remain faithful to God's mandate for social responsibility. Some are poets and song writers; still others have the gifts of governing and soldiering.

It is out of this earthy existence that Old Testament characters write their own stories of their discoveries of God in their midst. They compose psalms and hymns and spiritual songs. They wage war against the various forms of injustice they encounter. They sin and are forgiven; they sin and refuse to repent and are destroyed. Their daughters are married and bear children; others of them are raped and they seek revenge. In short, their experience is the same as many in urban centers whose motto is often "life is a bitch" and yet who find in these Old Testament stories a source of great hope.

But the attraction of the Old Testament does not diminish the New Testament. In the Gospels Jesus was clearly perceived as "one of the folks" by the common people. They heard him gladly (Mark 12:37). The Gospels are full of people trying to cope with the ordinariness of life—eating and drinking, marrying and burying, and trying to figure out the meaning in it all. Throughout all of this, and in the middle of it, Jesus lived and taught his followers how to think and feel about the God they believed in but could not find.

The epistles are also alive with significance for those carving out a practical theology. For twenty years prior to my present position at Fuller Seminary, I served congregations in Detroit. They had all grown out of the ministry of Berlin M. Nottage, an outstanding black evangelist. He had come to the city during the height of the depression years and was fired with a desire to "reach everyone in general and black people in particular." He and his colleagues pitched a tent in the black community, an area referred to locally as "black bottom." In the ensuing years six congregations developed and spread over much of the central city and into River Rouge. B. M. and his wife, Leah, invited me to live with them. For several years I ate at his table, traveled with him, and learned his mind about things.

Nottage was a fine preacher, a welcome speaker at many notable conferences and pulpits. But it was his heartbeat that captivated me. His passion was truly Pauline; he yearned to see the gospel preached and a people raised up for God's glory. He preached mostly from the Gospels and the epistles. He preached that in Christ, a favorite expression of Paul, people were finally and fully somebody, that in Christ black people were as near to God as was Jesus; that the sinful, the outcasts of society, were especially qualified for the new order. He delighted to explore the famous Pauline argument that "God chose the foolish things . . . the weak . . . the lowly . . . the despised . . . to nullify the things that are." (1 Cor. 1:27–28). Thus, the passion to preach the gospel and his yearning to see black people enabled by the grace of God became inseparable. It was always difficult to see where the seam between gospel and black culture was sewn.

Nottage taught these congregations from the epistles, especially Ephesians and Colossians, and built a biblical foundation grounded in what God, in Christ, had wrought for humankind. He was a dispensationalist for the most part, but it seemed to me that he used it as a useful framework from which he departed at will. This was especially true in his teaching about holiness of life and the work of the Spirit in healing. He knew that to feed these flocks, now being shaped by an entirely new environment, the city, he had to draw upon the entire text—Old and New. Yet that movement, which the late chronicler of revival, J. Edwin Orr, called one of the most remarkable outbreaks of revival he had seen in recent American church life, was anchored in the epistles, in the "mystery" revealed to the saints, in the revelation that in Christ there is a new humanity.

Nottage was a layman. He had been commended by the Christian Assemblies (Plymouth Brethren), but had no formal theological training. Furthermore, he saw in the Scriptures no distinction between clergy and laity. For these reasons he insisted that the gifts of the Spirit be recognized and exercised in the assembly. But he also knew that more formal training was needed if the work of God would endure over the years.

Theological reflection on the work of God among his people is an intellectual pursuit. It requires gifted persons whose intellectual gifts can be devoted to this task. Not everyone can do it; not everyone has the time. But as these gifts emerge they must be encouraged, set aside, and their insights incorporated into the church's life.

THE SCRIPTURES AND A NEW IDENTITY

God has a thing about names. The names he gives his people, from Adam and Eve to Peter and Paul and then on through to Revelation, are not random selections. Often the names he gives are synonymous with the character of those named. More importantly, those names are inextricably linked with the destiny of the tribe. Individuals have meaning only in relation to the greater meaning of the people, the whole nation. A good illustration of this is connected with the naming of the twins, Esau and Jacob, in the household of Isaac. Jacob was a conniver, a crook, a supplanter from his mother's womb.

Among the prophets we find Hosea suffering the tortures of an outraged husband when he hears Jehovah command him to call his beloved children names that indicate God's displeasure with Israel (1:2–9). The Old Testament is full of such illustrations. They reveal that God knows people through and through and is deeply concerned about what they are and what they could be. But it also shows that God has a larger redemptive purpose for the people.

Names can be changed. Jacob becomes Israel, and the whole race of rebellious and skeptical people who came out of Egypt—who were not a people—become the people of God, a royal priesthood, a holy nation. The lesson is clear: to encounter a holy God and to commit oneself to that God is not only to belong to him, but also to become like him. That means, of course, the most radical internal change imaginable. It is a transformation from rebellion and anarchy against God and from unknowable evil to obedience and unspeakable holiness. It is also a move from being an isolated person to becoming a member of a new household of faith. The psalmist enjoins the saints to rejoice in Jehovah who is a "father to the fatherless, a defender of widows . . . [who] sets the lonely in families . . . [and] leads forth the prisoners with singing" (Ps. 68:5–6). The image of a God who finds a homeland for the desolate is pregnant with meaning for the oppressed, and leaders in the

122

church must grapple with its meaning for discipling new converts from among the marginal peoples.

It is within these new "homelands" that new identities take shape. Individuals who were nobodies in their own eyes and in the estimation of others begin to take themselves seriously because God takes them seriously. The new community takes them seriously. Even a hostile society will begin to take them seriously, especially if their behavior begins to affect their lost neighbors.

When John and Vera Mae Perkins move into northwest Pasadena they are simply another family. But when, under their leadership, a new community consciousness emerges, then city hall has to take the community seriously. The police department must respond differently, and when they do, the drug dealers also have to take another look at the neighbors. That is when the fire bombs crash through the living room windows. But reform did not begin with demonstrations and speeches. It began with the reestablishment of community.

In community people are forced to see themselves differently, as God sees them. But seeing oneself differently in community is only the beginning. Since the individual in community and the community are together committed to a holy God, they are becoming like that God. And as Verkuyl points out, Jehovah is the God of change. Commenting on the difference between Jehovah and the gods of the nations, the noted missiologist observes that "the Baalim, nature gods, were the gods of the status quo. Jahweh is the God of the exodus, the God of liberation."[8]

The point is well taken and so is his further insight that the intention of Jehovah for his new people is also revolutionary.

> He intends to form a people that will live out His mercy and righteousness, a people who may in all their human relations give concrete shape and form to God's mercy and righteousness . . . the God of the exodus, the God who leads the march to freedom, keeps going through history. He does not stop until that goal is reached and the kingdom is realized, the kingdom in which righteousness covers and permeates the whole of life.[9]

The revelation that God moves into history and changes things is indeed radical, and it has serious implications for the believing community. For this reason the group must guard against anything that would compromise its single-hearted devotion to Jehovah. Paul, in seeking to pastor the church in Corinth, used Israel's experience with idolatry to call them to renewal. He capped his argument with the cryptic phrase, "Therefore, my dear friends, flee from idolatry" (1 Cor. 10:14).

By their impatience and unbelief, Israel clearly rejected their God. They had exchanged a living God who had already set them free for an image that was powerless to move them toward their true destiny. Such idolatry is a form of atheism. Idols have no power to effect change nor to move a people into the future. By abandoning Jehovah they also compromised their mission to be a light unto the nations, thus ensuring that their communal life would become ingrown and incestuous. The new community must be on its guard against all forms of idolatry.

It is one of the important callings of leadership to help the disciples identify the idols of their own time and place. Leaders must train the disciples in the art of defense against the allurements of idolatry. (See Paul's example in Corinth, 1 Cor. 8–10.) All efforts must be expended to protect the integrity of the community. Thus Jehovah proposed to Moses that a new beginning be made, and except for Moses's intercession and his keen sense of rightness before God, Israel's history might have been a different one (Ex. 32:7–14). Ananias and Sapphira were destroyed because of their lies, but the real lesson was the lengths to which God was willing to go in order to protect the integrity of the early church (Acts 5:1–10). If the solitary are to be safe, the homestead must have integrity.

To mention the ever-present threat of idolatry to the believing community is to realize that at the core of that community's life is worship. Worship is the essence of a life in God. It denotes a relationship with God that is both intimate and deeply respectful, a truth Jesus both expressed and taught his followers. The Lord's Prayer, the model for Christian worship, opens with such a reference to this relationship (Luke 11:2–4).

Worship is also the key to our humanity. Geoffrey Wainwright, in speaking of Jesus as the paradigm for the worship practice, observes that "the synoptic Gospels present Jesus as fully human to the depths of his being. The expression of this is the fact that he *prays*."[10] To be human is to pray; to pray is to be human. Prayer is communion, and this ability to commune with God is one of the constitutive elements in our humanity. It is an essential meaning of the *imago dei*, the image of God in humanity.

Furthermore, worship is the ordering of all aspects of the Christian enterprise. Wainwright puts it well in his attempt to unite doctrine and life with worship. He sees

> Christian worship, doctrine, and life as conjoined in a common "upwards" and "forwards" direction towards God and the achievement of His purpose, which includes human salvation. They intend God's praise. His glory is that He is already present and within us to enable our transformation into His likeness, which means participation in Himself and His kingdom.[11]

Wainwright says this in speaking to the need for a unified vision of worship: "Worship is better seen as the point of concentration at which the whole of the Christian life comes to ritual focus."[12] The ritual form will vary with each community, for even though many believers seem afraid of the term, they all have some preferred ritual form. But leadership should be sought that can bring together, in whatever form it takes, these key elements of doctrine, worship and life.

Another key element in the movement toward transformation is prayer. An effective movement, one that exerts a mighty influence, is always one that prays without ceasing. It is a prayerful people, seeming to live in the spirit of prayer. In this it is most like its founder who prayed always. Because he prayed, his disciples requested that he teach them to pray. Disciples, in whom is the Spirit of prayer, must nevertheless be taught how to pray.

There is no aspect of church life that expresses so much

sloppiness as prayer; no exercise that betrays more our spiritual ignorance; no other discipline that exposes more our bankruptcy of sound words. We must study the prayer life of the people whom God so greatly used in Scripture in order to tighten up our prayer life. The faithful use of the Psalms is crucial in this regard. It is imperative that leaders realize that their role is chiefly a priestly function—representing God among the people and representing the needs of the people before God. Failure here is to doom the entire enterprise. Failure here allows the assembly to fall into the hands of the stylists and hucksters.

People who are being transformed and who, because of this, are being a transforming presence in the world, also reveal a life in the Spirit. It is clear that at the end of this century the Holy Spirit is revealing himself to the people of God. Entire movements and new churches are being called into existence in all parts of the world without the baggage and other encumbrances of churches from other parts of the world. Such new works of God are not caused by human, but by divine power.

The Spirit is clearly universal, not the possession of any tradition or nation, and demonstrates a historic unwillingness to be enculturated or domesticated by Westerners. The Spirit is not necessarily clerical. The Spirit is not male, but often wears the face and form of women who preach and teach the good news and perform mighty deeds worthy of the book of Acts.

Transformation is the work of the Spirit of Christ (2 Cor. 3:17–18). Apart from the Spirit there is no possibility of change—whether one speaks of conversion or the ongoing work often referred to as sanctification. The same can be said of prayer, for the Spirit makes intercession for the church according to the will of God (Rom. 8:26–27) . The believer is enjoined to "live by the Spirit," to "walk in the Spirit," to be "led by the Spirit" (Gal. 5:16–25). The Christian is to pray in the Spirit (Eph. 6:18).

A study of the work of the Spirit is needed by many communions if they are to grasp the truly radical nature of their heritage in God. Furthermore, without renewal in the Spirit the church will simply fold under the clever onslaught of the wicked one. To attempt the transformation of any given turf is to encounter opposition, and that opposition is basically spiritual in nature. The church must engage this conflict with the weapons of righteousness if it is to haul down everything that opposes itself against the knowledge of God (2 Cor. 10:3–6). There can be little doubt that spiritual warfare must take a central place in the thinking of church leaders today. Any hang-ups about "signs and wonders" must be laid aside and theologians and ethicists, along with pastors and laity, must seek guidance for warfare in the Spirit. As the songwriter once put it, "The conflict of the ages . . . is upon us today."[13]

NOTES

[1]Jesse Jackson preached this same message among the poor in Marks during a visit in 1983 in support of Bobbie Jackson and other leaders running for public office.

[2]David Bosch, "Evangelism, Why the Endless Debate?" *The International Bulletin of Missionary Research* (July 1987): 101.

[3]John P. Meier, "Two Disputed Questions in Matthew 28:16–20," *Journal of Biblical Literature* (1977): 3.

[4]See Magnuson, *Salvation in the Slums.*

[5]See Vincent Harding's Introduction in Walter Rodney's, *How Europe Underdeveloped Africa* (Washington, D. C.: Howard Univ. Press, 1972), xxii.

[6]John De Cruchy, *Theology and Ministry in Context and Crisis: A South African Perspective* (Grand Rapids: Eerdmans, 1987), 65.

[7]Andrew Kirk, *Good News of the Kingdom Coming: The Marriage of Evangelism and Social Responsibility* (Downers Grove, InterVarsity, 1983), 97.

[8]Johannes Verkuyl and H. G. Schulte Nordholt, *Responsible Revolution: Means and Ends for Transforming Society*, trans. Lewis Smedes (Grand Rapids: Eerdmans, 1974), 12.

[9]Ibid., 13.

[10]Geoffrey Wainwright, *Doxology: The Praise of God in Worship, Doctrine and Life* (New York: Oxford Univ. Press, 1980), 21.

[11]Ibid., 10.

[12]Ibid., 8.

[13]A case needs to be made for this in light of the growing rituals of worship associated with alternative lifestyles and values alien to Judeo-Christian values. One thinks, for instance, of rituals associated with the resurgence of the Ku Klux Klan to forms of Satan worship with their ritual sacrifices, including "sacrifices" involving children.